Make a 2D RPG in a Weekend

With RPG Maker VX Ace

Darrin Perez

Make a 2D RPG in a Weekend: With RPG Maker VX Ace

ISBN-13 (pbk): 978-1-4842-1041-3

ISBN-13 (electronic): 978-1-4842-1040-6

Trademarked names, logos, and images may appear in this book. Rather than use a trademark symbol with every occurrence of a trademarked name, logo, or image, we use the names, logos, and images only in an editorial fashion and to the benefit of the trademark owner, with no intention of infringement of the trademark.

The use in this publication of trade names, trademarks, service marks, and similar terms, even if they are not identified as such, is not to be taken as an expression of opinion as to whether or not they are subject to proprietary rights.

While the advice and information in this book are believed to be true and accurate at the date of publication, neither the author nor the editors nor the publisher can accept any legal responsibility for any errors or omissions that may be made. The publisher makes no warranty, express or implied, with respect to the material contained herein.

Managing Director: Welmoed Spahr
Lead Editor: Ben Renow-Clarke
Technical Reviewer: Michael Lin
Editorial Board: Steve Anglin, Mark Beckner, Ewan Buckingham, Gary Cornell, Louise Corrigan, Jim DeWolf, Jonathan Gennick, Robert Hutchinson, Michelle Lowman, James Markham, Matthew Moodie, Jeff Olson, Jeffrey Pepper, Douglas Pundick, Ben Renow-Clarke, Dominic Shakeshaft, Gwenan Spearing, Matt Wade, Steve Weiss
Coordinating Editor: Christine Ricketts
Copy Editor: Michael G. Laraque
Compositor: SPi Global
Indexer: SPi Global
Artist: SPi Global

Distributed to the book trade worldwide by Springer Science+Business Media New York, 233 Spring Street, 6th Floor, New York, NY 10013. Phone 1-800-SPRINGER, fax (201) 348-4505, e-mail orders-ny@springer-sbm.com, or visit www.springeronline.com. Apress Media, LLC is a California LLC and the sole member (owner) is Springer Science+Business Media Finance Inc (SSBM Finance Inc). SSBM Finance Inc is a Delaware corporation.

For information on translations, please e-mail rights@apress.com, or visit www.apress.com.

Apress and friends of ED books may be purchased in bulk for academic, corporate, or promotional use. eBook versions and licenses are also available for most titles. For more information, reference our Special Bulk Sales–eBook Licensing web page at www.apress.com/bulk-sales.

Any source code or other supplementary material referenced by the author in this text is available to readers at www.apress.com. For detailed information about how to locate your book's source code, go to www.apress.com/source-code/.

*This book is dedicated to those who strive to make their dreams manifest.
Never give up on what your heart dictates!*

Contents at a Glance

About the Author xv

About the Technical Reviewer xvii

Acknowledgments xix

Introduction xxi

■Chapter 1: Laying Out the Framework 1

■Chapter 2: The Characters of Our Game 15

■Chapter 3: The Upper Catacombs of Eagle's Crossing 35

■Chapter 4: Populating Eagle's Crossing 61

■Chapter 5: The Lower Catacombs of Eagle's Crossing 81

■Chapter 6: The Caves 97

■Chapter 7: The Pixies' Forest (West) 123

■Chapter 8: The Pixies' Forest (East) 145

■Chapter 9: The Ancient Temple 165

■Chapter 10: What Comes Next 187

■Appendix: Useful Resources for 2D Game Creation 217

Index 221

Contents

About the Author xv

About the Technical Reviewer xvii

Acknowledgments xix

Introduction xxi

■Chapter 1: Laying Out the Framework 1

Story 1

Basic Game Play Considerations 3

The Town of Eagle's Crossing 4

The Adventurer's Quarter in Eagle's Crossing—A Minimalist
Item Shop 12

Of Blank Maps 13

Summary 13

■Chapter 2: The Characters of Our Game 15

Overview 15

Equipping the Characters 19

Some More Equipment-Related Talk 22

Pricing 22

Creating Your First Weapon and Armor 24

First the Axe… 24

…Then the Tunic 24

Equipping a Bow and Arrow 25

Creating a Character Select System 26

Summary 33

■**Chapter 3: The Upper Catacombs of Eagle's Crossing** **35**

Overview 35

The Upper Catacombs 36

    The Catacomb Key 39

    Of Damage Formulas and Spells 41

    The Enemies of the Upper Catacombs 45

    The Blocking Door 47

Creating Wall Tiles That the Player Can Pass Through 49

The Treasure Room 50

Creating Chests with Contents Dependent on Characters 53

Creating the Spell Scrolls 55

    Considerations 55

Eventing the Spell Scrolls 57

Summary 59

■**Chapter 4: Populating Eagle's Crossing** **61**

Populating the Equipment Shop 61

Populating the Pub 63

    Creating Our Companions 65

    Eventing Our Companions 66

    Creating the Dismissal NPC 68

    Creating the Innkeeper NPC 70

Populating the Magic Shop 71

Populating the Item Shop 72

Companions and Shops... **74**

　Creating the Return Item 75

　Creating a Return Portal 76

Connecting Eagle's Crossing to the Upper Catacombs **78**

The Town Greeter **79**

Summary.. **80**

■**Chapter 5: The Lower Catacombs of Eagle's Crossing**.................. **81**

The Lower Catacombs.. **81**

　What Does the Town Greeter Have to Say? 82

Level Overview.. **82**

Creating Transfer Events for the Upper Catacombs............. **83**

Static Encounters with Variable Enemy Troops **84**

Let's Create a Puzzle!.. **88**

　The Stone Tablets 88

　The Statues and the Gate 89

The Treasure of the Lower Catacombs.................................. **91**

The Living Statues.. **93**

Summary.. **96**

■**Chapter 6: The Caves** **97**

The Caves... **97**

　What Does the Town Greeter Have to Say? 98

　Level Overview 98

Creating Transfer Events for the Lower Catacombs **99**

The Enemies of the Caves **100**

　Random Roaming Enemies.. 103

Doors!.. 107

    Doors That Require Keys 107

    Doors That Open with Switches.. 109

The Cave's Treasure 113

    Random Treasure... 114

The Magic Oar 116

    The Magic Oar Chest Event.. 118

Kerberos, the Three-Headed Dog—Our First Boss.............................. 120

Summary 121

Chapter 7: The Pixies' Forest (West) 123

The Pixies' Forest (West)... 123

    What Does the Town Greeter Have to Say? 123

    Level Overview 124

Creating Transfer Events for the Caves 124

The Enemies of the Pixies' Forest (West) 125

    Ambush Encounters.. 127

    The Ambush Encounter Parallel Process Event 129

Unlocking the Pixies' Vale 130

    The Queen of the Pixies.. 134

    The Accessory Shop 139

    The Portal to Eagle's Crossing.. 140

The Treasure of Pixies' Forest (West) 142

The Path to Pixies' Forest (East)...................................... 143

Summary.. 144

■Chapter 8: The Pixies' Forest (East) 145

The Pixies' Forest (East) 145

What Does the Town Greeter Have to Say? 145

Level Overview 146

Creating Transfer Events for the Pixies' Forest 146

The Enemies of the Pixies' Forest (East) 147

Paired Encounters 149

Hidden Dwellings and Portals 150

The Magic Sail 151

Hidden Pixies 153

The Treasure of Pixies' Forest (East) 156

Lamia, the Snake Monster—the Second Boss.................... 156

Life After Lamia 161

Summary.. 163

■Chapter 9: The Ancient Temple.. 165

The Ancient Temple 165

What Does the Town Greeter Have to Say? 165

Level Overview 166

The Enemies of the Ancient Temple 167

The Dark Priests 170

The Lost Adventurers 171

Barrier to the End 173

The Braziers.. 173

The Wall of Fire.. 175

The Ancient Artifact 176

The Great Escape 179

    The Ancient Spirit 179

    Encountering the Ancient Spirit 179

    No Return, Yes Escape 183

Congratulations! 185

Summary 185

■**Chapter 10: What Comes Next** **187**

The Bazaar NPC 187

    Overview 187

    Shop Processing—Scripting Style 187

    Creating the Bazaar 191

    Finishing Up the Bazaar 193

The Next Leg of the Journey 195

A Portal Appears 195

Using the Portal 197

A Random Portal 199

    Spawning the Random Portal 200

    Quibbles 201

Handling Random Encounters with Common Events 202

Other Cool Things 205

    Another Way to Randomize Chests 205

    Day-Night Cycle 207

    Random Encounters in a Day-Night Cycle 210

    Achievements 213

Summary 215

■**Appendix: Useful Resources for 2D Game Creation** **217**

RMVXA Help Resources 217

Art Creation 218

Art Databases 218

Sounds and Music 219

Fonts 219

Other Game Engines 219

Closing Notes 220

Index **221**

About the Author

Darrin Perez (1988–) was born in Alexandria, Virginia, and currently resides in Puerto Rico. His debut fantasy novel, *Whispers of Dawn*, was written as a self-imposed challenge in the spirit of NaNoWriMo (National November Writing Month). He has also written many video game–related articles for HubPages and published an e-book concerning RPG Maker VX Ace (a video game development engine), which was later expanded and published by Apress under the title *Beginning RPG Maker VX Ace*. His latest nonfiction work, *Make a 2D RPG in a Weekend*, is his second book to be published by Apress.

About the Technical Reviewer

Michael Lin is an experienced RPG Maker developer and has created scripts for RPG Maker VX Ace since 2012. He is the founder of HimeWorks, a web site dedicated to resources for RPG Maker, which includes a wealth of scripts and tutorials on game development and programming.

Acknowledgments

The story of this book begins about the time that I was finishing *Beginning RPG Maker VX Ace*. Ben Renow-Clarke expressed interest in my writing a second book concerning the engine, a book a reader could follow through and finish within a single weekend. I immediately rose to the challenge and decided that the simplest type of game to make within the engine would be a dungeon crawler. It was then that I began to create the game and write the book in parallel. Afterward, we iterated upon the work, editing, formatting, and proofreading it to the levels of quality that Apress is known for. I have always enjoyed a good dungeon crawler. While they tend to be among the simplest role-playing games, there's also a chance to inject a surprising amount of complexity into them. In any case, that's enough about the book. You'll get to read it soon enough!

As is proper for the section, I would like to acknowledge the efforts of everyone at Apress who has worked with me, especially Ben Renow-Clarke, who ignited the spark that led to my writing this book, and Christine Ricketts, who has served as this book's coordinating editor—the glue that binds the project together, if you will. They have been quick to aid me when problems surfaced during the creation of this book. Honorable mention goes to Michael G. Laraque (copy editor) and Dhaneesh Kumar (formatting and composition). It is safe to say that, without the efforts of those working at Apress, this book would not be in your hands.

Michael Lin served as this book's technical reviewer (as he did for my last), and I would like to thank him again for helping me to make this effort the best it can be. He is quite the font of knowledge when it comes to RPG Maker VX Ace (RMVXA) and Ruby, and he is quick to catch any inefficiencies in event code and scripts alike.

I would like to thank the RMVXA community as a whole for all that they have done to make exploring and using RMVXA as easy as humanly possible. It has provided countless resources (both in the form of tutorials and other essential assets, such as sprites and music). Working with a game-development engine can be a daunting task, but the community is always willing to lend a helping hand to anyone in needs. It includes far too many people to name, but I hold them dearly in my heart.

On a personal note, I would like to thank my parents, Jose Perez and Victoria Diaz, who serve as my eternal bulwarks, allowing me to weather things that would otherwise break me. My closest friends are always there as well, to lend a hand whenever I need it.

Finally, I thank you, dear reader. At the end of the day, writers write for their audience. While there are many other factors that drive me to write, I can safely concur with the general thought that there's not much of a point in writing if your work is not read. Knowledge is not meant to be kept locked within a cabinet but, rather, released to the masses! So, get to it, and may you enjoy reading this book as much as I enjoyed writing it!

Introduction

Overview

Welcome to *Make a 2D RPG in a Weekend*! This book will take you through the process of using RPG Maker VX Ace (RMVXA) to make a six-level dungeon crawler within a single weekend. It will explain how to do what is necessary to create the game, so don't worry if you have had no prior RMVXA experience. With that said, if you have read my previous book, *Beginning RPG Maker VX Ace*, you'll have a leg up to work on this one. Here's a short list of things that were covered in my previous book relevant to this one.

- Events: How they work and how to create/edit them

- RMVXA's Map Editor: How to use it to add and edit maps

- RMVXA's Database: How to use it to add, delete, and edit entries.

Those are the bare essentials of using RMVXA. If you're anything like me, you'll probably learn how to do some or all of the above through mere experimentation. Anyway, let's move on to the next topic of interest in this introduction.

The Engine of Choice

You will have to use the full version of RMVXA to create this game. RMVXA (and a slew of related products, while we're on the subject) can be purchased from the official site at www.rpgmakerweb.com.

The exact link to download RMVXA is www.rpgmakerweb.com/products/programs/rpg-maker-vx-ace.

When not on sale, RMVXA usually costs $69.99, but you can try it for free for an entire month by grabbing the trial version. You will be asked for your name and e-mail address, if you attempt to download the full version of RMVXA (whether you pay for it at that time, wait until later, or decide not to keep using the product). If you use Steam, RMVXA is available through, and frequently on sale on, that platform as well.

Source Code Considerations

As you may have already noticed, this book's source code includes the full game and a few other things as well. Among the extras included are a set of blank maps for each of the six distinct dungeon levels covered in the book. It is my opinion that mapping is one of the more time-consuming aspects of RMVXA game design, so I included those maps as a shortcut if you want a head-start but don't want to be completely spoiled. You can see the game in its completed state and take as little or as much from it as you want. I merely ask that you take the time to go through the book and try to do as much of it as you can on your own. Making a game is like most other things in life: practice makes perfect.

Why Make a Dungeon Crawler?

A dungeon crawler is simple. The simplest dungeon crawlers break the standard role-playing game rule (if you will) of requiring a story. You can read some more considerations on the subject in the first chapter of this book.

Chapter 10

The book's final chapter exists outside the challenge posed by this book's title. Its proposes some interesting features that you can add to your game after you have officially completed it. Depending on your personality, time limits may be stressful, fun, or something in between. Thus, I didn't want you, the reader, to have to race to add to the game the extras discussed in Chapter 10.

CHAPTER 1

■ ■ ■

Laying Out the Framework

During the course of this chapter, we will be laying out the framework for our weekend game. This includes the story line, a general overview of each of our playable characters, and the basic foundation of our game's town. We will be creating the town area, but you can also find each of this game's maps in the book's source code.

Story

The first objective at hand in the creation of our turn-based, top-down dungeon crawler is to lay out our story. While dungeon crawlers are not usually pinnacles of complex storytelling, some still have at least a solid framework that carries their players through the game. Here are some examples of story lines (or absence thereof) in dungeon crawler role-playing video games, in no particular order of complexity.

- In *Rogue*, the classic dungeon crawler that inspired an entire genre (roguelikes), the player's only objective is to survive as long as possible. The dungeon is infinitely deep, and there isn't really a lore-related reason for the player's actions.

- In *Diablo* (technically an action role-playing game [RPG]), the player is an adventurer who arrives at the town of Tristram in an attempt to defeat the eponymous villain. Lore books within the dungeon lay out the backstory for the game's setting and context for certain areas.

- The remake of the very first *Etrian Odyssey* had a story mode that improved upon the mostly bare-bones plot of the original version. Even so, the basic framework of the plot is as follows: the player is a Highlander who arrives at Etria in search of fame, glory, and honor and eventually uncovers something that could jeopardize the entire town and even the rest of the world...

- *Eye of the Beholder* is a classic PC role-playing game that has a party of four adventurers trying to find and defeat a great evil under the sewers of the city of Waterdeep.

You may have noticed a common thread among most of those descriptions. Mainly, *the plot in a dungeon crawler is merely an excuse for the player to get into the dungeon and play!* Even so, that shouldn't stop you from adding plot to your dungeon crawler, as desired. Because most of the dungeon crawlers that I have played involve defeating a final boss, let's have one in which the player has to find an artifact hidden within the deepest levels of the dungeon. Here's a succinct blurb for our game's story line.

You are an adventurer from a faraway land who has arrived at the town of Eagle's Crossing. Legends speak of an ancient artifact buried deep within the town's catacombs. The artifact is said to have the power to heal any wound. Some even claim that it can raise the dead. It is owing to the last claim that you have made the arduous journey to the town, for you have lost **someone dear to you** recently.

I bolded the former words for the purpose of mechanics: I plan to have multiple playable characters. Thus, in a game, if you have different characters with different motivations, it only makes sense that the certain someone be different for each character.

■ **Note**   No one ever said you had to reveal *who* the character has lost. Maybe he/she lost multiple beings. Sometimes, the best plots are those that reveal only what is strictly necessary.

We'll honor the age-old tradition of classic dungeon crawlers and have three different characters representing classic fantasy archetypes.

- **Palnor** the *Warrior*: Palnor hails from the highlands directly south of the realm's northern mountains. His town was razed by one of the many mountain tribes. He seeks the ancient artifact in order to revive his kin and the rest of the people of his town. As a Warrior, Palnor has the widest weapon and armor selection of any of the three classes of characters, including the unique ability to wield two-handed swords and axes and heavy armor. However, he cannot master any spells.

- **Gust** the *Bandit*: Gust used to be as unsavory a character as one could imagine, and one most would rather not associate with, until the day he laid eyes on the princess of one of the desert clans. He swore thereafter to change his ways. However, his past life has caught up with him once again. He quests for the ancient artifact to revive the one person he has truly loved. As a Bandit, Gust is the only character who can use bows. His melee weapon and armor selection suffer a bit in comparison to those of the Warrior, but he makes up for it with the ability to cast low-level spells.

- **Feylia** the *Mage*: Graduated at the top of her class in the mystical arts, Feylia seeks the ancient artifact to revive her younger brother, who was lost in a terrible plague that struck the western lands when she was barely of age. As a Mage, Feylia has the worst weapon selection of any of the three characters. However, her spell book can carry any and all spells that she manages to find within the dungeon. Additionally, she is the only character who can wear magic robes. A well-equipped Mage is arguably the most fit for the dungeon's deeper levels.

With that out of the way, we pretty much have the skeleton of our plot. About the only thing left to do is provide more context to the town of Eagle's Crossing, as follows.

The town of Eagle's Crossing was created 411 years ago by a group of trading partners who wanted to live away from the various monarchies that would control them. Most of the olden kingdoms have since changed their methods of rule, but Eagle's Crossing remains the destination of choice for anyone who wishes to elude the less secluded parts of the world. Nestled against a mountainside that was carved out to form the town's catacombs, adventurers are now making their way to Eagle's Crossing in hopes of finding the artifact supposedly hidden within.

There you have it! The impetus for our players to start the game, summarized within a single page.

Basic Game Play Considerations

Dungeon crawler RPGs, more than any other type of RPG, live or die on their game play. After all, and as we have already demonstrated, you don't need much of a plot for a dungeon crawler. It is imperative, from the very start of your project, to think about what type of game play your dungeon crawler game will have. Here are some good questions to ask yourself.

- **Will I use RMVA's default battle system?** There's nothing wrong with using it. Then again, if you want to make a classic dungeon crawler, you might want enemies to move on the screen as you're fighting. In that case, you may have to tweak the system a little. Mind you, this does not necessarily have to involve heavy scripting.

- **How will the loot system work?** Many dungeon crawlers eschew the usual static treasure chests in favor of a more randomized system. This can result in some crazy things, such as getting the third-best sword in the game on the second floor. Such craziness has been largely circumvented over the years by the presence of loot tables that determine what can and cannot drop in a certain area. Another important consideration in the same train of thought is whether you will have the player find most of his/her items in the dungeon or have a town's shop stock some of them. In the latter case, gold (or whatever you would call your currency) gains value.

- **How will the leveling system work?** Most dungeon crawlers stay true to their RPG core. Thus, enemies offer experience, and the player's character (or characters) levels up once he/she has earned sufficient experience. On that note...

- **Will my dungeon crawler be a party-based or individual character game?** This is a really important question with no single correct answer. Citing as examples the games mentioned at the beginning of this chapter, *Rogue* and *Diablo* are controlled by a single character. *Etrian Odyssey* and *Eye of the Beholder*, on the other hand, are party affairs. As RPG Maker VX Ace (RMVXA) is designed to handle a battle party of up to four members, the easiest type of dungeon crawler to create with the engine is a party-based one.

- **Will my dungeon crawler have permadeath?** This is another important question, to which you should probably answer "no," unless you have a very specific reason to implement it in your game. *Permadeath* is short for "permanent death" and basically means that if characters die, they stay dead, with no way to be revived or otherwise allow you to use them in your party any longer. Most roguelikes include permadeath, which adds to their notorious levels of difficulty. They also have a single save game slot that deletes itself when the player dies, to prevent him/her from cheating death, as it were. Our game, on the other hand, will not have any of these mechanics.

- **Will the player be able to return to the town after leaving?** This correlates with earlier points of interest. If you want the player to live solely off of his/her own resources, you can bar access to the town after he/she leaves the first time. On the other hand, you wouldn't want to do this if you want the character to be able to use the town to sell his/her hard-earned loot and buy niceties.

Exactly how I implement game play will be explained throughout the book.

■ **Note** It's as good a time as any to point out that our game will not have a world map. The player starts in a town and goes into a linear dungeon that descends ever deeper into the bowels of the town.

The Town of Eagle's Crossing

As the sole representation of civilization present in our game, Eagle's Crossing will be our player's destination for rest, when he/she is not diving into the dungeon. The player will have access only to a specific part of Eagle's Crossing called the Adventurer's Quarter. It houses four buildings that provide for most of an aspiring dungeon crawler's needs. See Figure 1-1.

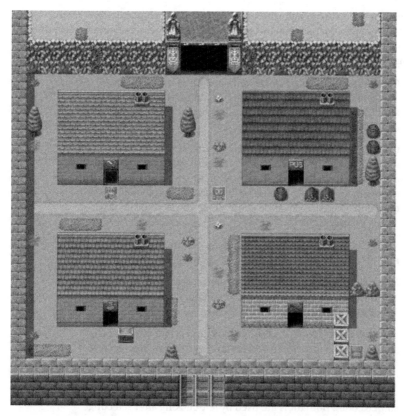

Figure 1-1. *A map of the Adventurer's Quarter in Eagle's Crossing, our game's safe zone*

The four buildings of Eagle's Crossing are (starting from the top left and going in a clockwise motion) are as follows:

- **The Equipment Shop**: Sells weapons and armor for use by the Warrior and the Bandit. The Mage is better served by shopping at the Magic Shop.

- **The Pub**: Every adventurer needs a place to kick back and relax when after returning from a particularly draining dungeon crawl. The pub serves as both a place to recruit companions and recover HP (health points) and MP (magic points).

- **The Magic Shop**: Sells equipment and spells for the Mage. The Bandit may also derive some benefit from visiting this shop, while the Warrior will probably give it a pass.

- **The Item Shop**: Sells consumable items and other miscellanea. All characters will want to visit this shop, if only to buy potions to restore HP and MP.

Perceptive eyes will also note the presence of a nonplayer character (NPC) at the lower-right corner of the town, seemingly blocked off from the rest of civilization. He'll be host to a particularly neat shop concept, but I'll get to that in the final chapter. The first order of business is to make the map, as displayed in Figure 1-1. Here's what you need to do:

- Create a new project, if you haven't already (I named mine DungeonCrawler), by clicking the File menu near the top of the application and then clicking New Project (you can press Ctrl+N, if you'd rather use hotkeys instead).

- Create a new map by right-clicking (or pressing Insert while hovering over) the project name at the lower-left corner of the screen (that part of RMVXA is the map list and is where our game's maps will go). Make sure that the new map has a width of 25 and a height of 25 and uses the Exterior Tileset. Name it "Eagle's Crossing."

- Verify that RMVXA is in Map Editing Mode (you can find the option in the Mode menu; alternatively, press F5).

- Directly below the menu bar, there are several series of icons. You'll want to find the series that has a pencil next to a square. Those are two out of five of RMVXA's map-drawing tools.

- Using either the pencil or the square tool (I prefer the pencil for single tiles and the square tool for larger groups of tiles, such as the roofs of our town's buildings), copy the map in Figure 1-1 (if the black and white is throwing you off, you can find blank versions of all of the maps in this game in the downloadable source code). Both tools are used by left-clicking after selecting the tile you wish to draw on the map. (With the square tool, you can also hold the mouse button and drag, to increase the size of your rectangle.)

- Once you are done with the exterior, you'll want to create the building interiors. With that said, take a look at the following note.

■ **Note** Using the sample maps provided within RMVXA is a great way to populate your game world. You can find them by right-clicking the map list at the lower-left corner of RMVXA and selecting the Load Sample Maps option.

That's precisely what I will be doing to create the building interiors. For a longer game, you'll probably want to dedicate a single map to the entirety of your town's interiors. Because this game will be designed in fewer than 20 maps (most of those will be consigned to the dungeon floors themselves), we can use one map slot per building. It doesn't matter much, all things being told. In any case, I tweaked the relevant sample maps, so that they would fit in a 17×13 tile space (this stops the map from scrolling while the player is on it). It gives the shops and the pub a neat little sense of coziness, in my opinion, anyway. Figures 1-2 to 1-4 contain the relevant screenshots. You'll notice the absence of the Item Shop among those screenshots, but I'm planning to do something neat with that near the end of the chapter. For the sake of consistency, I'll show the buildings in the same order as I noted them previously.

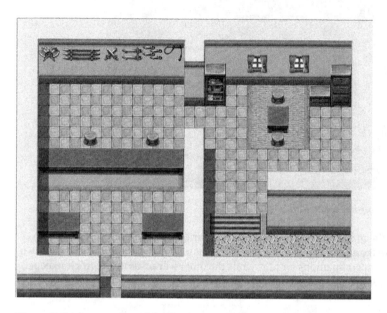

Figure 1-2. *A screenshot of the Equipment Shop*

Given that I wanted to condense the interiors into 17×13 tile spaces, the Weapon Shop sample map is better to work from than the Armor Shop (the Armor Shop is more spacious). I closed off the counter and added a second stool. This shop will have a pair of shopkeepers at the counter. One will deal in weapons; the other will deal in armor.

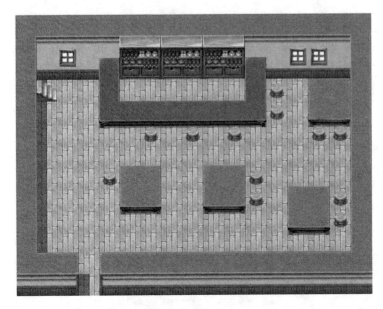

Figure 1-3. *A screenshot of the Pub*

The Pub is the map that I had to tweak most. I started with the InnF1F sample map and tweaked it to the state you see in the preceding figure. This building will also have two NPCs. One will offer companions for hire, while the other will act as the town's innkeeper, allowing the player to rest between dungeon crawls.

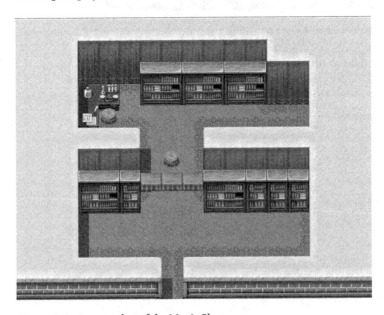

Figure 1-4. *A screenshot of the Magic Shop*

I used the Pencil Tool to move the more important parts of the Magic Shop to the center of the screen and then surrounded the shop with walls. Not much else to say about this one. A single NPC will be sitting on the stool closest to the entrance and will offer both spell scrolls and equipment best suited to the Mage.

■ **Tip**   The easiest way to copy large swaths of terrain is by holding down the right button on your mouse and dragging it to encompass the area you require. The resulting rectangle of tiles can be placed by left-clicking the map. I recommend using the Pencil Tool for this.

While our town is currently devoid of life, that will be changing soon. We're going to add some NPCs to our world. You'll have to do the following:

- Switch from Map Editing Mode to Event Editing Mode. You can either use the Mode menu or press F6 (the hotkey for Event Editing Mode).

- Once you're in Event Editing Mode, you can right-click any tile of the map to bring up a small menu with several options. Head on over to the Magic Shop and right-click the stool behind the counter. The option we want to click is New Event.

- Afterward, you will be greeted by a large screen with many options. For now, just double-click Graphic and select the NPC graphic that most appeals to you for a Magic shopkeeper. (Most of the human characters are contained in the graphics sets that are named Actor and People.)

- Repeat this process on the other maps to add four other NPCs in the following locations: two in the pub (behind the counter), and two for the equipment shop (again, behind the counter).

That's all well and good, but now we have to link each of the building interiors with its exterior. To do this, we must use transfer events. You can create a transfer event automatically (via the Quick Event Creation submenu that you receive when you right-click a map in Event Editing Mode) or manually. Also, there's a way to make a single transfer event that covers multiple locations. As you may have noticed when you created your first event, the Create Event screen defaults to a certain set of parameters. Walking Anim. (short for "Walking Animation") is toggled; the event Priority is set to Below Characters (meaning players can pass over the event square); and the event Trigger is set to Action Button, meaning that the player can activate the event by pressing Enter while in contact with the event. For Below Characters and Above Characters, the player is in contact when he/she is directly above/below the event. For Same as Characters, the player is in contact with the event when he/she is directly next to and facing it.

With all of that said, when I list event code during the course of this book, I will list any differences in starting parameters and then write out the actual contents of the events themselves. To add an event command to an event, all you have to do is right-click the @> symbol in the Contents section and select Insert. You will receive a three-page list of event commands that you can plug into any of your events. For example, following is a transfer event that connects the interior of the Equipment Shop to its exterior. Note how the event's contents are displayed with the @> symbol at the beginning. This is exactly how it would look inside RMVXA.

```
Trigger: Player Touch
@>Play SE: 'Move', 80, 100
@>Transfer Player:[001:Eagle's Crossing] (006,011)
@>
```

■ **Note** I used Quick Event Creation to make the event on the previous page. Note how automatic transfer events default to Player Touch instead of Action Button. As the name implies, such an event triggers when the player walks onto it (or into it, in the case of Same as Characters Priority).

Using that transfer event as a template, make the other two interior transfer events. Once you're done, you'll want to make the events for the exterior. This time, let's use one of my favorite transfer event trimming devices: the Parallel Process trigger. Events with a Parallel Process trigger are always running in the background, waiting to be activated. Be careful not to crash/hang your game with them! Anyway, click one of the corner squares of Eagle's Crossing and create a new event. This meta transfer event, if you will, is going to do the following:

- Determine the player's location by polling his/her x,y position and storing the data into a pair of variables. The Control Variables event command will handle this.

- Via the use of Conditional Branches (another event command), check to see if the player is standing at the entrance to one of the buildings.

- If he/she is, transfer him/her to the appropriate interior map.

Without further ado, here's the event:

```
Trigger: Parallel Process
@>Control Variables: [0019:X] = Player's Map X
@>Control Variables: [0020:Y] = Player's Map Y
@>Conditional Branch: Variable [0019:X] == 6
  @>Conditional Branch: Variable [0020:Y] == 10
    @>Transfer Player:[002:Weapon Shop] (004,011)
    @>
  : Branch End
  @>
```

```
: Branch End
@>Conditional Branch: Variable [0019:X] == 18
  @>Conditional Branch: Variable [0020:Y] == 10
    @>Transfer Player:[003:Pub] (003,011), Up
    @>
  : Branch End
  @>
: Branch End
@>Conditional Branch: Variable [0019:X] == 18
  @>Conditional Branch: Variable [0020:Y] == 19
    @>Transfer Player:[004:Magic Shop] (007,011), Up
    @>
  : Branch End
  @>
: Branch End
@>
```

■ **Tip** Another way to go about this is through the use of regions. You would have to use Get Location Info in conjunction with a third variable, to store the region value of the square the player is standing on. Then, you use a distinct region for each building entrance. I will be using regions in a later chapter, but for the most part, you'll want to pick up my *Beginning RPG Maker VX Ace* (Apress 2014) to read more about them.

If we were to use a region for the same effect, part of the Parallel Process event would look something like the following code (keep in mind that you need to actually mark the Equipment Shop entrance with the correct region, or nothing will happen):

```
@>Control Variables: [0019:X] = Player's Map X
@>Control Variables: [0020:Y] = Player's Map Y
@>Get Location Info: [0018], Region ID, Variable [0019][0020]
@>Conditional Branch: Variable [0018:Region] == 1
  @>Transfer Player:[002:Weapon Shop] (004,011)
  @>
: Branch End
@>
```

As long as you're not planning to use the regions for something else (and, given that you have 63 possible regions, this should not be an issue), it could be a nice way to handle area transitions. Now, what happens if you want to embrace even more minimalism in your game and don't want your buildings to have actual interiors?

The Adventurer's Quarter in Eagle's Crossing— A Minimalist Item Shop

That's a bit of a mouthful for a section title, isn't it? Anyway, this section will tackle the opposite approach. We're going to create an Item Shop that consists merely of a single event that handles what would normally be handled by NPCs inside the building. On that same note, the Item Shop won't have an interior. We want this event to do the following:

- Make the player's sprite disappear (to simulate the effect of going into the building).

- Bring up a description of the shop and its keeper(s). For subsequent visits, you could make it so that said description is abbreviated a bit.

- Give the player a list of choices. In the Item Shop, the choices would be Shop and Leave.

- Once the player is done, have him/her leave the shop and make his/her sprite reappear.

- Otherwise, revert to the previous list of choices, so that the character can continue shopping.

If you want to try your hand at the event, here is what it will require in terms of raw event commands and setup.

- Change Transparency

- Show Text

- Show Choices

- Shop Processing

- Set Move Route

- Jump to Label/Label

- The event should have a Below Characters priority and a Player Touch trigger.

That shouldn't be too hard to work out. If you figured it out and want to check against what I did, or are otherwise stumped, take a look at the following to see the relevant event code. Do note that we have yet to design what kinds of items our game will have. As that will be covered later on, I'm using comment placeholders for the event. You'll want to place this event directly on top of the entrance to the Item Shop.

```
Trigger: Player Touch
@>Change Transparency: ON
@>Text: -, -, Normal, Bottom
:      : You enter the shop and are instantly overwhelmed by
:      : the variety of equipment available. You look at your
```

```
:       : gold bag as you make your way to the counter, where
:       : an older shopkeeper awaits.
@>Label: MainMenu
@>Text: -, -, Normal, Bottom
:       : What can I do for you?
@>Show Choices: Shop, Leave
: When [Shop]
  @>Comment: Shop Processing Goes Here.
  @>Jump to Label: MainMenu
  @>
: When [Leave]
  @>Set Move Route: Player (Wait)
  :                 : $>Turn Down
  :                 : $>Transparent OFF
  :                 : $>1 Step Forward
  @>Text: -, -, Normal, Bottom
  :      : You leave the shop.
  @>
: Branch End
@>
```

There you have it! The label is used to ensure that the player is not kicked out of the building as soon as he/she leaves a shop. By doing it this way, we make it so that the player has to consciously leave the shop. You could do the same thing for each of the other buildings as well, if you're so inclined.

Of Blank Maps

As mentioned at the start of the chapter, the source code for this book includes the entire game. If you're ever stumped by how I implemented X or Y, feel free to take a look. Additionally, if you'd rather not draw up the area maps yourself, I provide blank versions of every single map used for the game in the same project file. Drawing maps for your game is good practice but one of the most time-consuming aspects of working with RMVXA. Because the intent of this book is to create and complete a game within a weekend, don't hesitate to use the blanks to accelerate your progress, if need be. That concludes this chapter.

Summary

During the course of this chapter, we started work on our game, establishing the basic plot of the story, the playable characters, and creation of the basic skeleton of Eagle's Crossing. The town will be populated in Chapter 4. In the next chapter, we will create our game's main characters and a way for the player to select which to play the game as.

CHAPTER 2

The Characters of Our Game

This chapter is all about our three characters and the many systems related to them. During the course of this chapter, I will cover subjects such as the stat system that we will use for our game, a list of weapons and armor that will be available, and a way for the player to pick which character he/she would like to use.

Overview

The first order of business is to decide how we want our stat system to work in our dungeon crawler. By default, RPG Maker VX Ace (RMVXA) favors high numbers. For example, a character can have up to 9999 HP (health points) and 999 MP (magic points). However, most of the dungeon crawlers I mentioned in the previous chapter run with much lower numbers. For instance, *Diablo*'s characters have one primary stat that can be increased to 255 and three secondary stats with lower caps. So, in the interest of differentiating our game a little more from RMVXA's default system, let's lower our stats by a lot. Doing this will also help us simplify the game in ways that possibly won't be apparent for quite a while. First, head to the Database and erase the preexisting entries for everything in the Classes and Actors tabs of the Database. You can find the Database from the Tools menu at the top of the application or by pressing F9.

Tip A really easy way to purge a Database section is by changing the section's maximum entries to 1. You can do this by clicking Change Maximum near the bottom of most Database tabs. Then, you need only reset the value to the maximum of your choice, right-click the lone remaining entry, and then click Clear (or press Del) to delete it.

After you are done with the purge, head over to the Classes tab. Let's create the classes for our three playable characters. First, we need to figure out each class's starting stats, as well as how much of each stat we want them to gain at each level. As I mentioned, I want the stat system to have *low* numbers. Right now, all of the stat curves are high.

Take a look at Table 2-1 to see how low I'm going. MHP and MMP are abbreviations of Maximum HP and Maximum MP respectively. The other abbreviations are as follows:

- ATK – Attack

- DEF – Defense

- MAT – Magic Attack

- MDF – Magic Defense

- AGI – Agility

- LUK - Luck

Table 2-1. *List of Base Stats for Each Class and the Stats That They Gain on Each Level Up*

Class	MHP	MMP	ATK	DEF	MAT	MDF	AGI	LUK
Warrior (base stats)	50	0	3	3	1	1	1	1
Warrior (stats per level)	6	0	1	1	0	0	0.5	0.5
Bandit (base stats)	35	15	2	2	2	2	2	2
Bandit (stats per level)	4	2	0.5	0.5	0.5	0.25	1	1
Mage (base stats)	20	30	1	1	3	3	1	1
Mage (stats per level)	2	4	0.25	0.25	1	1	0.5	0.5

As you can see, the Warrior starts with the most HP but no MP, while the Mage starts with the least HP and the most MP. The Bandit's stats are between those of the other two classes. Note how each class differs in its stat gains and its initial stats. Taking the Warrior class as an example, here's how you can set up/change its stats:

- Double-click any of the eight parameter curves, and a new window will open, containing the base curve. Keeping in mind that RMVXA can plot a custom stat curve, all you need to know is the character's stat value at 1 and 99, based on stat growth.

- Click Generate Curve, and you'll get a window much like Figure 2-1 (which illustrates the Mage's HP curve). In the Warrior's case, he has 50 HP at Level 1. For Level 99, he will have leveled up 98 times for 6 extra HP a level, or 588 more HP. So, the Warrior will have 638 HP at a hypothetical Level 99.

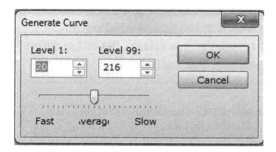

Figure 2-1. *A screenshot of the Generate Curve window for the Mage's MHP stat*

■ **Note** The slider bar below the curve values determines the speed at which the class gains that particular stat. You can make classes that gain the bulk of a stat early in their career and others that gain it later on. For the purposes of this game, leave all of these sliders on the default setting of Average.

- Plug in 50 for Level 1 and 638 for Level 99, and you're set! Now, I could have you crunch all of those other max parameters, but that would be mean. So, instead, see Table 2-2 for a list of the maximum stats for each of the three classes at Level 99.

Table 2-2. *The List of Maximum Stats for Each Class at Level 99*

Stats at Level 99								
Class Name	MHP	MMP	ATK	DEF	MAT	MDF	AGI	LUK
Warrior	638	0	101	101	1	25	50	50
Bandit	329	218	51	51	51	26	100	100
Mage	216	422	25	25	101	101	50	50

With those numbers in hand, take some time and fill out the stat blocks for each of the three classes. After that, we have one last curve to work on: the experience curve. By clicking the button marked "..." below Exp Curve, you'll bring up a screen with various parameters that can be changed with scrolling bars. Minimize all of them (which drops Base Value and Acceleration B to 10 and the other two parameters to 0) for the three classes and then note how the experience required per level has dropped.

■ **Note** A quirk of dropping all four parameters to their minimums is that experience requirements to gain a level beyond level 84 *drop* rather than increase. This isn't significant, given our game's level cap; it's just a neat little bit of trivia that I noticed.

The last thing we have to do in the Classes tab is set up the features of each class. See Table 2-3 for a list of features that each class should have.

Table 2-3. *A List of Features for Each of the Game's Three Classes*

Class Name	HIT%	CRI%	Equip Weapon	Equip Armor	Add Skill Type
Warrior	85	5	Axe, 2H Axe, Dagger, Sword, 2H Sword	Light Armor, Medium Armor, Heavy Armor	No
Bandit	85	5	Axe, Bow, Dagger, Sword	Light Armor, Medium Armor	Magic
Mage	75	5	Dagger, Staff	Light Armor	Magic

■ **Tip** You can add and edit class Features by right-clicking a preexistent feature or, in the empty slot directly below the last feature in the list (the very first slot, if the Feature list is completely empty), by selecting Edit. Double-clicking works as well.

Now, flip over to the Actors tab and create your three characters. First, add their sprites and portraits, as seen in Figure 2-2.

Figure 2-2. *(From left to right) Palnor's sprite and portrait, Gust's sprite and portrait, and Feylia's sprite and portrait*

■ **Note** You can find Palnor's sprite in the Actor3 sprite set and his portrait in the similarly named portrait set. Gust's graphics are located under Evil, while Feylia's are in Actor2.

Next, we will fill out the General Settings for each actor as follows:

- **Palnor**: Class: Warrior—Initial Level: 1—Max Level: 20—Description: He seeks the ancient artifact in order to revive his kin and the rest of the people of his town.

- **Gust**: Class: Bandit—Initial Level: 1—Max Level: 20—Description: He seeks the ancient artifact in in order to revive the love of his life.

- **Feylia**: Class: Mage—Initial Level: 1—Max Level: 20—Description: She seeks the ancient artifact to revive her brother, lost to a plague years before.

In filling out the General Settings, you may have noticed the Starting Equipment section of the Actors tab. I'll get to that in a bit.

Equipping the Characters

For now, we'll want to come up with the armor and weapons that the player will find and use during the course of a play-through. It's not necessary to add all of the items to the Database just yet, but your game will benefit greatly from thinking about this and adding at least the first set of equipment. For starters, this will help you balance the stats of any enemies that the player will face in the first few levels of the dungeon. With that said, Table 2-4 covers the various weapon types that the Warrior and Bandit will be able to use (the Mage's staff-type weapons [staves] are a bit different, and I'll cover them momentarily).

Table 2-4. *The Four Types of Weapons Available for Warriors and Bandits to Use*

Swords	Damage	2H Damage
Base	2	3
Improvement per tier	2	3

Axes	Damage	2H Damage
Base	3	4
Improvement per tier	3	4

Daggers	Damage	
Base	1	
Improvement per tier	2	

Bows	Damage	Arrows
Base	2	1
Improvement per tier	2	1

The table bears a little explanation. Mainly, our game will have six types of materials for weapons. Those materials are (in order of damage potential): wood, copper, bronze, iron, steel, and mythril. The base potential damage of a weapon is the amount of ATK (attack) given by a wooden version of that weapon. For each tier higher than Wood, you add the improvement value. So, a mythril sword would give the wielder 12 ATK. 2H is shorthand for "two-handed." (It's a common nomenclature in role-playing gaming communities, so you might have already known that.) Only Palnor the Warrior is allowed to use two-handed swords and axes, which have roughly 50% more ATK than their one-handed cousins. Only Gust the Bandit is allowed to use bows, and they inflict extra damage if you have an arrow equipped in the off-hand slot (the one used for shields by default in RMVXA). Feylia's staves are a bit different in that they increase her ATK like other weapons, but they also increase her MAT. Additionally, there are only four types of distinct staff-type weapons. Obsidian is in the same tier as iron is for other weapons, while crystal is the same as for mythril. See Table 2-5.

Table 2-5. *The Four Types of Staff Weapons That Feylia Can Use*

Staves	ATK	MAT
Wood	4	2
Stone	6	6
--	--	--
Obsidian	10	14
--	--	--
Crystal	14	22

Armor is a little more complex than weapons. For one, mythril, in our game (and in certain fantasy settings throughout the years), is a magical metal that's unusually light. Thus, it is possible to make from it a tunic that even Feylia can wear. In the same vein, Palnor can wear any type of armor. Gust can wear light and medium armor, while Feylia can only wear light armor. The first five tiers of heavy armor are full plates (that is to say, they're a full suit of armor). Thus, Palnor cannot wear a helm while wearing any of those suits. Adamantine, in our game, is an exceedingly heavy metal that offers unparalleled protection, should you have the strength to wear it. No one was/is crazy enough to try and make weapons out of that particular metal. Adamantine comes in both chestplate (which allows a helm to be worn) and full plate varieties. See Table 2-6 for a full list of DEF values for our game's armor.

Table 2-6. *List of Armor and Helms Available in the Game*

Light Armors	Protection	Light Helms	Protection
Cloth Tunic	2	Cloth	1
Leather Armor	3	Leather	2
Studded Leather Armor	4		
Mythril Tunic	12		
Medium Armors	**Protection**	**Medium Helms**	
Chain Hauberk	9	Chain	4
Iron Chestplate	12	Iron	5
Steel Chestplate	15	Steel	6
Mythril Chestplate	18	Mythril	7
Heavy Armors	**Protection**	**Heavy Helms**	
Copper	8	Adamantine	8
Bronze	12		
Iron	16		
Steel	20		
Mythril	25		
Adamantine Chestplate	25		
Adamantine Full Plate	33		

Before we continue, let's go to the Terms tab and make changes to some of the sections. First, purge the Elements, Weapon Types, Skill Types, and Armor Types boxes of their contents. Next, fill them out, per Figure 2-3. (You can edit a term by left-clicking a field and then writing in or editing the appropriate name.)

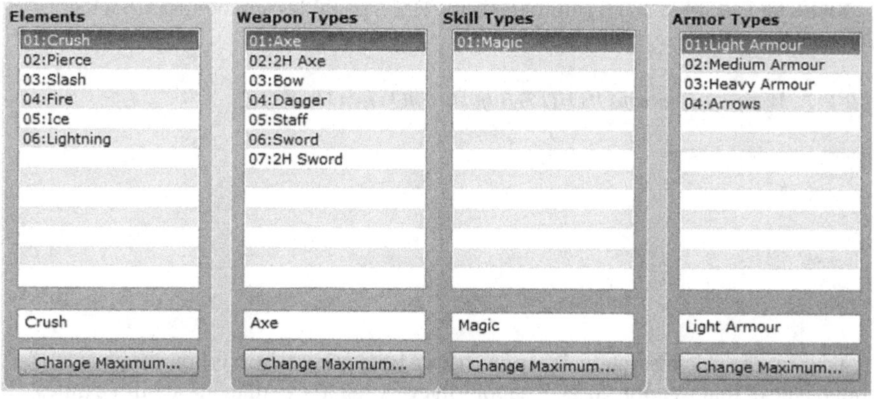

Figure 2-3. *A screenshot of the terms for the game*

You can see in the terms shown in the figure some design decisions I hadn't mentioned yet. I split Physical into three distinct types of damage. This allows us to make enemies that are resistant to a type of physical attack, while being vulnerable to another type. As for magical elements, I dropped them down to merely three, for the sake of simplicity. As noted in Tables 2-3 and 2-4 this game will have seven weapon types. As for

Armor Types, you might be surprised to see arrows make up a category there, but that is the easiest way to have an off-hand item in RMVXA.

Some More Equipment-Related Talk

Before you actually sit down to add the weapons and armor to the Database, there are some other considerations concerning them.

Pricing

How much gold will each piece of equipment cost? The easiest way to determine this is to price each similar item identically (give all one-handed weapons of the same tier the same price and do the same for two-handers as well). Of course, that would imply that all of the items are the same. In our game, axes do more damage than swords, which do more damage than daggers. One way to keep things fair is to have weapons modify the wielder's HIT% when used. HIT% is short for "Hit Rate" and determines with what frequency an attack connects with its target. Each of our three characters has a natural HIT% declared in their Features list. Weapons and armor in RMVXA can also contain features. When you give a piece of equipment the HIT% Feature, it modifies the user's HIT% by the declared amount. One-handed swords would be the middle ground, with no HIT% change. Axes would give the player a penalty to HIT%, while daggers grant a bonus. Two-handed weapons would give the wielder a HIT% penalty (stacking, in the case of axes). Feylia's physical attacks are already the weakest of those of the three classes, so let's make staves a neutral HIT% weapon.

Take a look at Table 2-7; it summarizes the HIT% penalties and bonuses that I am talking about.

Table 2-7. *Weapon Type and Its HIT% Adjustment When Used*

Weapon Type	HIT% Change
Sword	0
2H Sword	-5
Axe	-5
2H Axe	-10
Dagger	5
Bow	0
Staff	0

Now, for the pricing system. Weapons have a base price, which is how much a wooden type of that weapon costs. Weapons in every tier above that one are three times more expensive. Once again, staves are a bit different. See Table 2-8 for the breakdown.

Table 2-8. *Cost of Each Type of Weapon, Depending on the Material It Is Made Of*

Weapon Type	Cost (by tier)
Sword, Axe	20, 60, 180, 540, 1620, 4860
2H Sword, 2H Axe	40, 120, 360, 1080, 3240, 9720
Dagger, Bow	15, 45, 135, 405, 1215, 3645
Staff	20, 180, 1620, 15000

In addition, bows come slightly cheaper than one-handed swords and axes, because they require the added expense of arrows, to be fully effective. Arrows (not displayed in the preceding table) cost two-thirds the price of a bow of the equivalent tier. So, a wooden arrow would cost 10, a copper arrow 30, and so forth. As for armor (displayed in Table 2-9), pricing is a little more fluid. The reason for this is that it is subdivided into body armor and helmets. Thus, we have to control the pricing a little, lest it spiral out of control. Also, we have to price heavy armor accordingly, given that it consists (with the sole exception of the Adamantine Chestplate) of full suits that disallow the use of a separate helmet. Last, helmets (Table 2-10) cost half the gold of the body armor they complement. An iron helm costs 540 gold, for example.

Table 2-9. *The Cost of Armor in the Game*

Armor	Cost
Cloth Tunic	10
Leather Armor	30
Studded Leather Armor	90
Mythril Tunic	1500
Chain Hauberk	270
Iron Chestplate	540
Steel Chestplate	1080
Mythril Chestplate	2160
Copper Fullplate	100
Bronze Fullplate	300
Iron Fullplate	900
Steel Fullplate	1800
Mythril Fullplate	3600
Adamantine Chestplate	4320
Adamantine Fullplate	7200

Table 2-10. *The Cost of Helmets in the Game*

Helm	Cost
Cloth Cap	5
Leather Cap	15
Chain Helm	135
Iron Helm	270
Steel Helm	540
Mythril Helm	1080
Adamantine Helm	2160

With all of that set up, you are ready to add each of the weapons and armor to the Database, but not before I show you how.

Creating Your First Weapon and Armor

As I tend to note when asked, "RMVXA is nothing if not intuitive." Thus, adding and deleting things from the Database is as easy as can be. Take a moment to purge the Weapon and Armor tabs of the Database. Once you're done, change the maximum of the Weapons tab to 40 and the Armor tab to 43. I'm going to guide you through creating a wooden axe and a cloth tunic.

First the Axe...

Head over to the Weapons tab and click the first Weapon slot on the left-hand portion of the screen. If you have erased everything beforehand, you should see a whole lot of nothing. Let's start by filling out the General Settings section:

- **Name**: Wooden Axe

- **Item** (by "Item," I mean items, weapons, and armor) icons draw from a special set of graphics. Double-clicking the Icon square will reveal the set. If you click any of the graphics, you will see the value of Index change. If you want to use the same axe graphic that I do, it is at Index 144.

- **Description**: A strange axe made out of wood.

- **Weapon Type**: Axe

- **Price**: 20

- **Animation**: 019: Blow Physical

Next, let's move on to the Parameter Changes section, where you need only give the wooden axe an ATK of 3. No other parameters are changed. As for Features, make the wooden axe's Atk Element Slash and a HIT of -5%.

...Then the Tunic

Switch to the Armor tab and click the first Armor slot on the left-hand portion of the screen. As before, let's start by filling out General Settings:

- **Name**: Cloth Tunic

- **Icon**: Index 168

- **Description**: Basic clothing for the average human of the world. Only offers the most basic of protection.

- **Armor Type**: Light Armor

- **Price**: 10

- **Equip Type**: Body

As for Parameter Changes, the cloth tunic will grant 2 DEF, and nothing else. The tunic is also functionally featureless. (It has a 0% EVA by default, which I left in for the sake of having something there, because why not?)

See, that wasn't so bad! Now, you can work on adding the other weapons and armor yourself. Feel free to choose the icons that you most like, as that's hardly important for the purposes of this book. Before I close out this section, you'll want to see Table 2-11 for a list of the Attack Elements of each of the different weapon types.

Table 2-11. *A List of the Attack Elements of Each Weapon Type in Our Game*

Weapon Type	Attack Element
Axe	Slash
Greataxe	Slash
Bow	Pierce
Dagger	Pierce
Staff	Crush
Sword	Slash
Greatsword	Slash

■ **Note** Atk Element is another Feature and, as such, can be added to both weapons and armor. In our game's case, I'll only be adding it to weapons. Simplicity is best.

When adding the items to the Database, you'll quickly notice that there will be space left over in the Armor tab, but that's intentional, as we'll be adding a few things to it during the course of this book.

■ **Note** Don't hesitate to take a look at the source code for help, if you want to see some more of the items in a completed state.

So, what about the bow and arrow thing, you may wonder? Check the next section for a display of how we're going to make it work.

Equipping a Bow and Arrow

The bow is easy. We just treat the bow like any other weapon, and we're set. How about the arrow? You might be thinking: I could just set the bow to allow Dual Wielding. If you do that, then the player could equip Gust with two bows. As amusing as that mental image is, let's not do that. How about giving only Gust the ability to equip arrows? It's a valid idea. After all, he *is* the only one of the three characters that can use bows in the first place. However, if you do *that*, the player can equip a dagger (or sword or axe, for that matter) in the main hand and an arrow in the off-hand. Quite the quandary, isn't it? Take a look at Figure 2-4 to see how we solve it.

Figure 2-4. A screenshot of the Wooden Bow and the property that allows its wielder to equip Arrows

Mainly, we make it so that bows allow their wielder to equip arrows as well (it's one of the weapon Features; you can see it on the right-hand side of Figure 2-4). Had we made arrows a weapon type rather than an armor type, we would have to enable Dual Wielding, which allows the loophole I warned against previously. Done in this way, we don't have to give Gust the ability to equip arrows (he'll gain the ability to use them for as long as he has a bow equipped), which closes the other loophole.

Now you should have your weapons and armor set, and your bows should have the correct Feature interaction with arrows. With that arduous task completed, we can now give our three characters some starting equipment. Head back to the Actors tab and allocate the starting equipment like so: Palnor should start with a copper sword and a cloth tunic, Gust should start with a copper dagger and a cloth tunic, and Feylia should start with a wooden staff and a cloth tunic.

Creating a Character Select System

Every good RPG that allows a choice of characters begins with a character select screen. It would be a bit jarring if you were to pick your character after the game had already started, after all. During the course of this section, we'll be creating a way for the player to choose which of the three characters he/she wishes to play as. Broadly speaking, there are two ways to allow the player to select a character.

- Use eventing on a special map.

- Use scripting to create a special Scene that holds a character creation menu.

As this is a weekend project, we'll be doing the former, which will take minutes, as opposed to the latter, which can take hours, unless you already have some amount of Ruby savvy and know-how. To complete this exercise, you will require the following:

- A new character that exists only while the player is choosing a character to play.

- A map containing the player's starting position and three events, one for each of the game's distinct characters.

- An Autorun event on that map, giving the player instructions on how to select a character.

- Once a character has been selected, we fade out the screen, give some exposition, and then transfer the player to Eagle's Crossing.

- At Eagle's Crossing, we will have to add an Autorun to fade in the screen after the transfer and give the player a small number of items and some gold to start with.

Let's go in order. Make your way to the Actors tab and select a blank slot in your Actors list (I chose slot 4). The only important aspect of this particular actor is its sprite graphic, but we'll give it a name too, for clarity, if nothing else. See Figure 2-5 for the graphic used for our actor, named Spirit. (You can find it in the !Flame graphic set; it's the blue flame with a full set of sprites.)

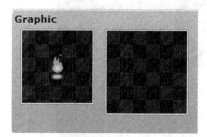

Figure 2-5. *The sprite used for the new actor. Note the lack of a portrait*

Next, I created a new map at the default size of 17×13 with the Dungeon template. The name of the map itself is irrelevant, so feel free to name yours as you choose. Then, I added a large central platform, as well as three smaller platforms. On each platform, I placed an event with the graphic of one of our three player characters. I then placed a single event at the top-right corner of the map (where the player would be unable to reach it) with an Autorun trigger. The solitary event has two pages. The second page is blank, with an Action Button trigger, and requires that self-switch A is on.

■ **Note** Think of a switch as a variable with only two possibilities: on and off. A self-switch is just that, but isolated to a single event. For example, you could make it so that when the player opens a chest, one of that chest's self-switches (RMVXA allows four self-switches per event) is flipped on, preventing the chest from being opened again. The value of a self-switch in one event has no effect on any other event, whether on the same map or on a different one.

The first page contains two Show Text commands, as well as a Change Menu Access command (which is set to Disable; we do this so the player can't open the menu while selecting a character). After those three commands are executed, we have the event set self-switch A to on. Take a look at Figure 2-6, to see a screenshot of what I have described.

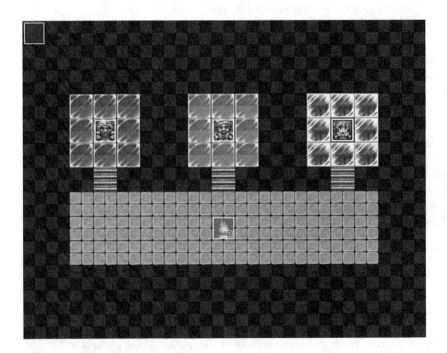

Figure 2-6. A screenshot of the character select map, from which the player starts the game

Page 1 of the Autorun event
Trigger: Autorun
@>Text: -, -, Normal, Bottom
:   : What course will you choose, sojourner? Choose the
:   : path you will walk on!
@>Text: -, -, Normal, Bottom

```
:     : \C[3]Move the Spirit to a character and press the Action
:     : Button to receive general information about them.
@>Change Menu Access: Disable
@>Control Self Switch: A =ON
```

Page 2 of the Autorun event

```
Condition: Self Switch A is ON
Trigger: Action Button
Leave the Contents section empty.
```

■ **Caution** If you don't break out of an event page that has the Autorun trigger, you will cause the game to loop it infinitely, forcing you to reset the game. In this particular case, you could use Erase Event to the same effect as the self-switch setting.

Each of the three character graphics has an event page of its own. Read on to see each of the character's relevant event codes.

Palnor

```
Priority: Same as Characters
@>Text: -, -, Normal, Bottom
:     : \C[2]Starting Stats:
:     : \C[18]HP: 50 \C[1]MP: 0
:     : \C[0]High HP, ATK, DEF growths. Can use most weapons and
:     : all armor. Cannot use spells, staves, or bows.
@>Text: -, -, Normal, Bottom
:     : Do you wish to choose Palnor the Warrior?
@>Show Choices: Yes, No
: When [Yes]
  @>Text: -, -, Normal, Bottom
  :     : Let your journey begin!
  @>Control Switches: [0001:Palnor] = ON
  @>Fadeout Screen
  @>Change Party Member: Add [Palnor]
  @>Change Party Member: Remove [Spirit]
  @>Text(S): Speed 2
  :          : You are Palnor the Warrior. Palnor hails from the
  :          : highlands directly south of the realm's northern
  :          : mountains. His town was razed by one of the many
  :          : mountain tribes. He seeks the ancient artifact in
  :          : order to revive his kin and the rest of the people
  :          : of his town. Rumor has it that it is located deep
  :          : within the bowels of Eagle's Crossing...
  @>Transfer Player:[001:Eagle's Crossing] (012,021), Up
  @>
: When [No]
```

```
  @>Text: -, -, Normal, Bottom
  :      : Choose wisely, sojourner…
  @>
: Branch End
@>
```

Gust

```
Priority: Same as Characters
@>Text: -, -, Normal, Bottom
:      : \C[2]Starting Stats:
:      : \C[18]HP: 35 \C[1]MP: 15
:      : \C[0]High AGI and LUK growths.
:      : Can use one-handed weapons and bows.
@>Text: -, -, Normal, Bottom
:      : Cannot use two-handed swords, axes, or staves.
:      : Cannot use high-level spells.
@>Text: -, -, Normal, Bottom
:      : Do you wish to choose Gust the Bandit?
@>Show Choices: Yes, No
: When [Yes]
  @>Text: -, -, Normal, Bottom
  :      : Let your journey begin!
  @>Control Switches: [0002:Gust] = ON
  @>Fadeout Screen
  @>Change Party Member: Add [Gust]
  @>Change Party Member: Remove [Spirit]
  @>Text(S): Speed 2
  :          : You are Gust the Bandit. Gust used to be as unsavory
  :          : a character as one could imagine, and one most would
  :          : rather not associate with, until the day he laid
  :          : eyes on the princess of one of the desert clans. He
  :          : swore thereafter to change his ways. However,
  :          : his past life has caught up with him once again. He
  :          : quests for the ancient artifact to revive the one
  :          : person he has truly loved. Rumor has it that it is
  :          : located deep within the bowels of Eagle's
  :          : Crossing…
  @>Transfer Player:[001:Eagle's Crossing] (012,021), Up
  @>
  : When [No]
  @>Text: -, -, Normal, Bottom
  :      : Choose wisely, sojourner...
  @>
: Branch End
@>
```

Feylia
```
Priority: Same as Characters
@>Text: -, -, Normal, Bottom
  :      : \C[2]Starting Stats:
  :      : \C[18]HP: 20 \C[1]MP: 30
  :      : \C[0]High MP, MAT, and MDF growths. Can only use staves
  :      : and daggers. Can only wear light armor.
@>Text: -, -, Normal, Bottom
  :      : Can use all spells.
@>Text: -, -, Normal, Bottom
  :      : Do you wish to choose Feylia the Mage?
@>Show Choices: Yes, No
 : When [Yes]
   @>Text: -, -, Normal, Bottom
   :       : Let your journey begin!
   @>Control Switches: [0003:Feylia] = ON
   @>Fadeout Screen
   @>Change Party Member: Add [Feylia]
   @>Change Party Member: Remove [Spirit]
   @>Text(S): Speed 2
   :             : You are Feylia the Mage. Graduated at the top of her
   :             : class in the mystical arts, Feylia seeks the ancient
   :             : artifact to revive her younger brother, who was lost
   :             : in a terrible plague that struck the western lands
   :             : when she was barely of age. Rumor has it that it is
   :             : located deep within the bowels of Eagle's Crossing.
   @>Transfer Player:[001:Eagle's Crossing] (012,021), Up
   @>
   : When [No]
   @>Text: -, -, Normal, Bottom
   :       : Choose wisely, sojourner…
   @>
 : Branch End
@>
```

As you can see, each of the three distinct character selection events has various similarities. In all of them, we have the game replace our indistinct Spirit with the chosen character, once the player has decided on who he/she wishes to use. Additionally, a switch named after the chosen character is set to on (which can be used to great effect, if you want to have conversation options that differ according to the character the player is adopting). No matter what character is chosen, the player is transported to Eagle's Crossing at the end of said event. Last, we add an Autorun event to Eagle's Crossing that handles the player's arrival at the town. This Autorun is slightly different, depending on the character the player has assumed. The code below remains the same, no matter which character is chosen.

■ **Note** While a full list of items will not be given until Chapter 4, you should take a moment to populate the Database with the two items listed in the following code, if only not to have to revisit this event later on. The Lesser Healing Potion has a Price of 10 gold and heals 35 HP, while the Lesser Magic Potion costs 20 gold and restores 30 MP.

```
@>Fadein Screen
@>Text: -, -, Normal, Bottom
:        : You arrive at Eagle's Crossing after many days of
:        : hard travel. With little more than your trusty
:        : weapon and fifty gold pieces to your name, you
:        : start your quest.
```

The following code differs according to the character chosen.

If Palnor
```
@>Change Items: [Lesser Healing Potion], + 3
@>Change Gold: + 50
@>Change Menu Access: Enable
@>Control Self Switch: A =ON
```
If Gust
```
@>Change Items: [Lesser Healing Potion], + 2
@>Change Items: [Lesser Magic Potion], + 1
@>Change Gold: + 50
@>Change Menu Access: Enable
@>Control Self Switch: A =ON
```
If Feylia
```
@>Change Items: [Lesser Healing Potion], + 1
@>Change Items: [Lesser Magic Potion], + 2
@>Change Gold: + 50
@>Change Menu Access: Enable
@>Control Self Switch: A =ON
```

■ **Note** For the code differentiation discussed earlier, you can use three distinct event pages or have a single page with conditional branches for each of the three possible characters. In either case, you'll still want to have another page with a non-Autorun trigger that requires that self-switch we toggled to be on. Make sure that page is the last one in the event.

Summary

During the course of this chapter, I covered many concepts concerning our game's three playable characters. These include their base stats and stat growths, their equipment permissions, and a special map that serves as our game's character-selection screen. In the next chapter, we will start work on our game's dungeon.

CHAPTER 3

The Upper Catacombs of Eagle's Crossing

Whereas the previous chapter covered our characters and created a basic selection system from which the player could choose, this chapter will cover the start of the dungeon crawl. In this chapter, we're going to design our game's first level.

Overview

The dungeon is the meat of a dungeon crawler game. The town exists only as a way station where the player can restore his/her resources in between trips. So, it's about time that we actually start work on the dungeon, right? First of all, we have to decide how many levels we want the game's dungeon to have. Six is a nice number to start with, so we'll go with that. Next, we must figure out what *zones*, if any, the dungeon will be divided into. For example, *Etrian Odyssey* is divided into five distinct zones (called stratums) of five floors each (as well as a sixth postgame stratum containing an extra five floors). Our game will have four different zones.

- **The Catacombs**: They will make up the first two levels of the dungeon. The Upper Catacombs will be Level 1 and the Lower Catacombs Level 2.

- **The Caves**: They will compose the next level of the dungeon.

- **The Pixies' Forest**: This part of the dungeon will make up Levels 4 and 5 of our game.

- **The Ancient Temple**: This is the last level of the game, in which the player will find the hidden artifact.

This chapter will cover the first level of the catacombs. So let us begin.

The Upper Catacombs

The catacombs were created centuries ago to serve as a resting place for the dead of a higher...calling. Kings, nobles, and other people of high rank were interred there. Living slime and smaller vermin have overrun the once sacred grounds. It is there that your adventure begins.

That's a little flavor blurb for the first dungeon level of our game. The first order of business is to map out our first level and populate it with treasure, enemies, and even a simple puzzle. Create a new map that is 40×32 in size, with the Dungeon1 BGM and a Cobblestones1 & Stone1 Battleback. You can do this by right-clicking (or pressing Insert while hovering over) the project name (or a preexisting map) in the map list section of RPG Maker VX Ace (RMVXA; lower-left corner). Then, see Figure 3-1 for a screenshot of the Upper Catacombs of Eagle's Crossing.

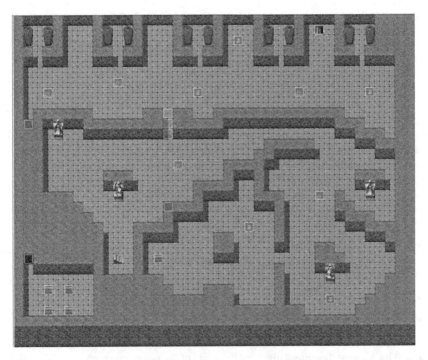

Figure 3-1. *A screenshot of the first floor of our dungeon. The upward staircase at the bottom left leads back to town*

■ **Note**   An easy way to set apart dungeon levels of a particular zone is to give them a distinct graphical style. The style I'll use for the catacombs (with a certain exception on the second floor) uses the Wall (Temple) tile for walls and the gray Cobblestones tile for the floor.

The screenshot's walls have been altered to improve visibility in the black-and-white versions of this book. You can see the original tileset by looking at the map within the source code download.

While I have provided a screenshot of the finalized map, it would still be good to talk about the map design process. Much like most other aspects of game design, practice will make perfect. Here is how I tackle my maps in RMVXA.

- **Step One: Brainstorm ideas for possible map elements.** This part of the map-creating process is purely conceptual. In the case of our first level, I wanted to have a simple floor that introduces the new player to the concept of the dungeon crawler. The Upper Catacombs contain several roaming encounters with Slimes and Rats, the two weakest enemies of our game. It also has a chest containing a key that will open the door blocking access to the second floor, as well as a secret passage for the perceptive.

- **Step Two: Draw up the basic terrain map**—in RMVXA, I mean. You can use the drawing tools near the top of the editor (the series of five icons that starts with a pencil and ends with a gray circle) by entering Map Editing Mode (pressing F5 or selecting it from the Mode submenu in the menu toolbar), selecting your tile of choice, and left-clicking while using your chosen drawing tool. In other words, this step is the map equivalent of creating an outline when writing a book. You should draw the major defining features of your map (using the tiles contained within the A tab) at this time.

- **Step Three: Add doodads.** Doodads are the little things that add variety to what would otherwise be a stale map. You can find doodads in tabs B and C of any given tileset. This map has coffins and statues that may or may not serve a greater purpose later on.

- **Step Four: Add events.** After the terrain has been mapped out with the Map Tool, we use the Event Tool to cover the rest. Remember that you can add events to your maps by changing to Event Editing Mode (pressing F6 or selecting it from the Mode submenu), right-clicking the square on which you wish to add the event, and selecting New Event (alternatively, you can left-click the square and press Enter). In the case of this map, we add several roaming encounters, as well as treasure chests and transfer events.

■ **Tip** Here's a tip related to drawing up terrain in RMVXA. The default visible area in an RMVXA game is 17×13. All terrain should be drawn with that in mind. When I was an RMVXA novice, I would make maps that had way too much empty space in them. You want the player to have a view similar to that shown in Figure 3-2, in which the immediate area is populated with walls and statues.

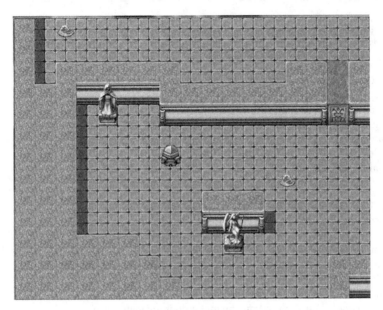

Figure 3-2. *A screenshot of the game in progress, showing Palnor in the early parts of the first dungeon level*

The general idea is that your player should never go through large expanses of area without finding a doodad or some other notable piece of terrain (exceptions to this could be a featureless desert or a blasted wasteland). I highly recommend that you play through some classic 2D role-playing games (RPGs), such as the oldest of the *Final Fantasy* or *Dragon Warrior* games, to see how their maps are designed. It will help you get a feel for your own mapmaking. If you must insert a large corridor, it should be as thin as possible, with turns here and there to break up the monotony. Score bonus points if you give the corridor significance (that is, unless you're making a literal maze, in which case, you don't want to make a bunch of corridors that lead nowhere). As already hinted at, the level has many twists and turns. It's quite possible to make a dungeon that has entirely square rooms, but it will be fairly dull, unless you make the rooms really small (because of the aforementioned empty expanses).

Take some time to draw and populate the first dungeon level. Once you are done with that, read on. What we're going to do now is add the level's events. Broadly speaking, there are fewer than ten distinct events on this map. Let's list them.

- We need an event for the treasure chest containing the key that opens the catacomb door.

- The door itself will be created with an event.

- We need four events, one for each of the treasure chests in the secret room.

- We need events to represent the Slimes and others for the Rats. However, you only really need one of each, as you can use copy and paste to duplicate each as many times as necessary.

- We need an event to handle the stair transfer events.

- We need a pair of events for the secret passage leading to the extra chests.

The Catacomb Key

As you might imagine, our first order of business is to create the key and our first two enemy types. Normally, when working through a level for a game, you want to create all of the assets that will be used within it first. Then, you can just add the relevant events in one go. First, let's create our key. Head over to the Items tab in the Database (you can access the Database quickly by pressing F9), expand the maximum cap to 40, and then use slot 36 for the Catacomb Key (the reason for the strange numbering will become clear as we keep working on the game). See Figure 3-3 for a view of the item in question.

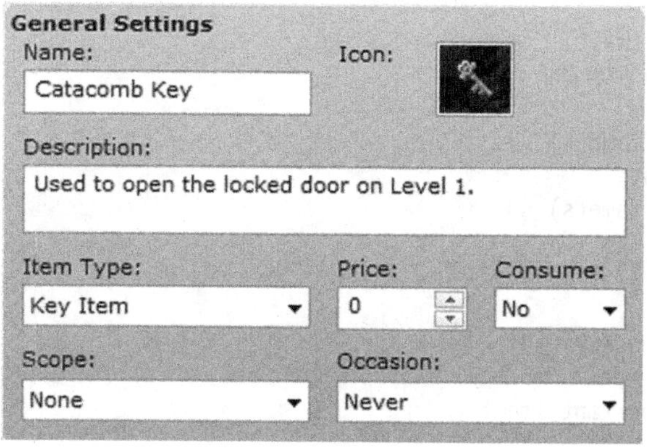

Figure 3-3. A screenshot of the Catacomb Key

We don't want the key to be sold or used up, so we set its Price to 0 and the Consume property to No. Because we don't want the player to use this particular item except when the game automatically does (when opening a certain door), we set Scope and Occasion to None and Never, respectively. You can use the Quick Treasure Chest Event to create the chest containing the Catacomb Key. This quick event is easily accessed by finding the Quick Event Creation submenu in the menu opened after right-clicking a map square while in Event Editing Mode. Then, highlight the submenu with your mouse pointer, and several options will appear. Click Treasure Chest (or, alternatively, press Ctrl+3 after left-clicking the map square on which you wish to add a Quick chest) and you're done! Of course, given that finding the key is an important achievement, we could reward the player with some experience points. 25 EXP should be plenty. You can use the Change Experience and Show Text event commands to tell the player that he/she has gained experience points. Here's the treasure chest event for the Catacomb Key. For both of the event pages, tweak every option given in the following code, as needed. You can right-click the Contents section of the event window to add a new event command or edit a preexisting command.

■ **Note**   The faster way to insert the treasure chest code is to create a Quick Treasure Chest and then edit it accordingly.

Page 1 of 2
Graphic: Closed red treasure chest in the upper-right corner of the !Chest graphic set.
Options: Direction Fix
Priority: Same as Characters
Trigger: Action Button
Contents:
```
@>Play SE: 'Chest', 80, 100
@>Set Move Route: This event (Wait)
:                     : $>Direction Fix OFF
:                     : $>Turn Left
:                     : $>Wait: 3 frame(s)
:                     : $>Turn Right
:                     : $>Wait: 3 frame(s)
@>Control Self Switch: A =ON
@>Change Items: [Catacomb Key], + 1
@>Text: -, -, Normal, Bottom
:       : Received \C[2]Catacomb Key\C[0]!
@>Text: -, -, Normal, Bottom
:       : You have found an important item!
@>Play SE: 'Skill3', 80, 100
@>Text: -, -, Normal, Bottom
:       : You have gained 25 EXP!
@>Change EXP: Entire Party, + 25
@>
```

Page 2 of 2
Graphic: Open red treasure chest three tiles below the upper-right corner of
the !Chest graphic set.
Condition: Self Switch A is ON
Options: Direction Fix
Priority: Same as Characters
Trigger: Action Button
No Contents

I placed this treasure chest by its lonesome a few squares to the east of the staircase
leading back to Eagle's Crossing.

Of Damage Formulas and Spells

Before we can work on the enemies in this first level, there is something more
immediately important to cover. We must decide what our game's damage formulas for
physical attacks and spells will be. Keep in mind that we lowered our game's stats by a lot,
so the default formula is far too much. Namely, a.atk*4 - b.def*2. To give an example
of this formula at work, say that we have an initial monster with an ATK of 10, and the
player character has a DEF of 5. We would be taking 30 HP of damage per hit. That would
kill Feylia in one hit, and the other two possible characters in two. As you can see, that's a
bit much for our game, given that we want to have lower stats across the board. So, what
formula will we use? A common convention of dungeon crawlers is to make it so that
every attack that lands results in at least one point of damage. To keep it simple, attack
and defense will correlate on a 1:1 basis in our game. That is to say, if the player has an
attack equal to his/her enemy's defense, he/she will deal 1 damage. Players deal damage
equal to the attack advantage that they possess. So, if the player has a 10 ATK and strikes
at an enemy having a 4 DEF, he/she will deal 6 damage.

With all of that said, head over to the Skills tab and find the Attack skill (the very first
one in the list) and change the formula from its default to the following:

```
a.atk > b.def ? a.atk - b.def : 1
```

If you have some Ruby experience, you will recognize the preceding as a ternary
expression. For those of you who don't know what that is, it is another way to express an
if/then relationship. The preceding could be written out as follows:

- if a.atk > b.def

- then a.atk - b.def

- else 1

So, if the attacker has more ATK than the defender has DEF, he/she inflicts damage
equal to the difference between his/her ATK and the defender's DEF. Otherwise, the
player inflicts a single point of damage. Using the previous example (monster ATK of 10,
player DEF of 5), our player would only take 5 HP of damage per monster attack. This is
a lot more manageable. For magic, we'll have similar formulas, with the caveat that we
will be designing enemies to have far less MDF than they have DEF. That helps to balance

41

the fact of Feylia having to use MP for her stronger attacks, in contrast to Palnor and Gust, who can use physical attacks to much greater effect. While we're on the topic of spells, take a look at Table 3-1, to see the list of spells that Gust and Feylia share.

Table 3-1. *The List of Spells That Gust and Feylia Can Both Cast*

Spell Name	Element	Description	Scroll Cost	MP Cost	Damage Formula
Fire	Fire	A spell that causes low Fire damage	30 G	2 MP	`2 + a.mat > b.mdf ? 2 + a.mat - b.mdf : 1`
Ice	Ice	A spell that causes low Ice damage	30 G	2 MP	`2 + a.mat > b.mdf ? 2 + a.mat - b.mdf : 1`
Lesser Heal	None	A spell that restores a low amount of HP	15 G	2 MP	`10 + a.mat*1.0`
Purge	None	A spell that cures the effects of poison from the target	30 G	2 MP	N/A
Return	None	A spell that returns the caster to town	30 G	10 MP	N/A
Shock	Lightning	A spell that does low Lightning damage	30 G	2 MP	`2 + a.mat > b.mdf ? 2 + a.mat - b.mdf : 1`

■ **Note** I will cover how to create the Return spell effect in Chapter 4, when we create a consumable item with the same effect.

Of course, Feylia wouldn't be much of a spellcaster if she didn't have some spells of her own. In the interest of economy of space, I'll provide the rest of her spell list in Tables 3-2 and 3-3. I'll be covering how to enter these spells into the Database in the next few pages.

Table 3-2. *First Part of the List of Spells That Only Feylia May Use*

Spell Name	Element	Description	Scroll Cost	MP Cost	Notes/Damage Formula
Blaze	Fire	A spell that causes moderate Fire damage	150 G	4 MP	`5 + a.mat*1.5 > b.mdf ? 5 + a.mat*1.5 - b.mdf : 1`
Bolt	Lightning	A spell that causes moderate Lightning damage	150 G	4 MP	`5 + a.mat*1.5 > b.mdf ? 5 + a.mat*1.5 - b.mdf : 1`
Chill	Ice	A spell that causes moderate Ice damage	150 G	4 MP	`5 + a.mat*1.5 > b.mdf ? 5 + a.mat*1.5 - b.mdf : 1`
Heal	None	A spell that restores a moderate amount of HP	75 G	4 MP	`20 + a.mat*2`
Sleep	None	A spell that may put its target to sleep	75 G	5 MP	90% success rate.
Blizzard	Ice	A spell that causes heavy Ice damage to all enemies	500 G	8 MP	`10 + a.mat*3 > b.mdf ? 10 + a.mat*3 - b.mdf : 1`

Table 3-3. *Second Part of the List of Spells That Only Feylia May Use*

Spell Name	Element	Description	Scroll Cost	MP Cost	Notes/Damage Formula
Cleanse	None	A spell that removes all negative effects from the target	150 G	6 MP	N/A
Greater Heal	None	A spell that restores a large amount of HP	225 G	8 MP	`30 + a.mat*3`
Immolate	Fire	A spell that causes heavy Fire damage to all enemies	500 G	8 MP	`10 + a.mat*3 > b.mdf ? 10 + a.mat*3 - b.mdf : 1`

(continued)

Table 3-3. *(continued)*

Spell Name	Element	Description	Scroll Cost	MP Cost	Notes/Damage Formula
Poison Cloud	None	A spell that may poison all enemies	300 G	10 MP	70% success rate.
Sleep Wave	None	A spell that may put all enemies to sleep	225 G	10 MP	90% success rate.
Thunder Storm	Lightning	A spell that does heavy Lightning damage to all enemies	500 G	8 MP	10 + a.mat*3 > b.mdf ? 10 + a.mat*3 - b.mdf : 1

Of course, all this talk of spells begs the question: How do we give Gust and Feylia their spells? The easiest way is to edit the appropriate Skills lists (that's a section in the Classes tab for each individual class created) and grant them at certain level intervals. You could have Gust learn his spell allotment at Level 5. Feylia would start the game with those spells. At Level 5, Feylia could learn the second tier of magic spells (Blaze through Sleep in Table 3-2). Then, she could learn every other spell when she reaches Level 10. The harder way will be discussed much later in the chapter, as an additional exercise. (Hint: It involves using scrolls.) Purge the Skills tab, except for Attack and Guard, and then take some time to add the 18 spells to the Database, before moving on. Following are some tips that will help you to create them correctly:

- The Damage section of the Skills tab contains the damage type (which also includes HP and MP recovery, so it's useful for healing skills as well), element (this is where you would put Fire, Ice, or Lightning), damage formula (where you can put the formula for a spell, where applicable), Variance (which I set to 0 for *all* spells), and Critical (which determines whether or not a skill can do critical damage; I set that to Yes for every spell with a damage formula).

- For spells that inflict a status effect, you set said status effect via the Effects section. A right-click (or double left-click) will bring up the Effects menu, which has many effects that can be added to a skill. What you're looking for is the Add State Effect. Then, you need only change the percent chance of the state being applied to the one listed in the previous tables (so, 70% for poison, and 90% for sleep).

- Scope is self-explanatory, in most cases. The one exception in the entire list of spells is Return, which should have a scope of None.

- Occasion is also fairly simple. Spells that deal damage (or inflict negative status effects) to enemies should only be usable **In Battle**. Return should be used **only from the menu** and every other spell should **always** be usable.

- The Using Message section is neat, if you wish to customize the message shown by the game when the player uses a spell. However, for the sake of expediency, I just use the "casts *!" button for each spell, to set the relevant message automatically.

■ **Note**   Make sure to give Feylia her six starting spells. As mentioned previously, that can be done through the Skills section of the Classes tab. Set the Level to 1, so that Feylia has immediate access to these spells.

The Enemies of the Upper Catacombs

Now, I will discuss the first two monsters of our game. As we want them to appear on the dungeon's first level, it stands to reason that we cannot make them too strong, lest they wipe out our player as soon as he/she starts playing. That would not be fun at all. Table 3-4 has a helpful breakdown of the monsters' stats and their damage type. Table 3-5 lists the experience and the gold the player receives when defeating the monsters.

Table 3-4. *Stats and Attack Element for the Slime and Rat Monsters in Our Game*

Name	MHP	MMP	ATK	DEF	MAT	MDF	AGI	LUK	HIT%	EVA%	Attack Element
Slime	5	0	4	1	1	1	1	1	75	0	Crush
Rat	8	0	7	2	1	1	3	3	80	5	Pierce

Table 3-5. *Experience and Gold rewards for the Slime and Rat*

Name	EXP	G
Slime	1	2
Rat	2	3

■ **Note**   Unless otherwise specified, I will use the self-named battle sprites for each enemy in our game. So, the Slime enemy uses the stock Slime graphic, and the Rat uses its own graphic.

Both of those monsters use only the Attack skill. Note that we didn't really provide our game's armor any special properties with regard to elemental resistances and/or weaknesses. I will cover that later in the chapter, when I discuss accessories in the dungeon. Remember: We're trying to keep the game as simple as possible. Make your way to the Enemies tab in the Database and plug in the stats for both enemies accordingly. Name and Parameters (MHP, MMP, etc.) are General Settings. HIT%, EVA%, and Attack Element are Features. You can set an enemy's experience and gold in the Rewards section, and usable skills are set in the Action Patterns section. Because every enemy defaults to using the Attack skill, no changes are necessary for our two enemies in that respect.

Next, switch over to the Troops tab. Here, we're going to create two troops: one for each enemy type (otherwise, we'd have no way of creating the event encounters). To create a new troop, do the following:

- Find the scrollable list of enemies in the right-hand portion of the Troops menu.

- Left-click the enemy you would like to add to the troop and then click ➤ **Add**.

- You can manually name the troop or have RMVXA auto-name it.

For later levels, we'll have troops of multiple enemies, but for now, just have a troop with a single Slime and another with a single Rat. After all of that, it's actually pretty easy to add the roaming encounters to the map. To make a roaming monster encounter that minds its own business until the player runs into it (or inadvertently runs into the player), use the following parameters.

Autonomous Movement
```
Type: Random
Speed: 3: x2 Slower
Freq: 3: Normal
```
Priority: Same as Characters
Trigger: Event Touch
Graphic: Slime or Rat as needed (Slime can be found in Monster2 and Rat in Monster3)

Contents
```
@>Battle Processing: <troop> (where <troop> is the selected Troop; in this
case, Slime or Rat)
: If Win
  @>Erase Event
  @>
: If Escape
  @>Set Move Route: This event
  :                   : $>Wait: 300 frame(s)
  @>
: Branch End
@>
```

■ **Note**   You could always just fall back to RMVXA's default random encounter system, easily accessible within a map's Properties menu. I'm just taking the opportunity with this game to use a less commonly used encounter system. There isn't really a right or a wrong way to create encounters in RPGs. It's all a matter of taste.

That's it! Because you want multiple Slimes and Rats on the map, you can copy and paste the original events accordingly. We want the encounters to re-spawn at some point, so that the player can use them to get stronger and gain more experience if he/she so desires. So, if the player wins, we erase the event temporarily. When **Erase Event** is used, the affected event ceases to exist, until the player leaves the map. (Events will also re-spawn if the player saves the game and reloads. This is a quirk that can be controlled via the use of scripting or heavy eventing. Consider this as a challenge that you can undertake when you gain more experience with RMVXA. So, when the player returns to this level, he/she will find that the monsters have returned as well.

■ **Note**   You could also use a self-switch conditional on a second event page, to remove the monster permanently after it is defeated. In that case, you would replace Erase Event with Control Self Switch. Just keep in mind that the players have to have a way to gain more experience and gold, or they might find themselves unable to get past a certain point.

The Blocking Door

Next, we must create the door sealing off the northern part of the catacombs. Because we want the player to obtain the Catacomb Key before being able to open the door, the door event will have two pages. Figure 3-4 will contain the details for page 1 of the door event. Figure 3-5 will contain the details for page 2 of the door event.

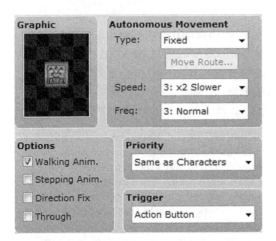

Figure 3-4. *Details for page 1 of the door event*

Page 1 of 2
Contents
```
@>Text: -, -, Normal, Bottom
:      : You see an ornate door. It has a strangely shaped
:      : keyhole.
@>
```

Page 2 of 2
Condition: Item 036:Catacomb Key exists
Contents
```
@>Play SE: 'Open1', 80, 100
@>Set Move Route: This event (Wait)
:              : $>Turn Left
:              : $>Wait: 3 frame(s)
:              : $>Turn Right
:              : $>Wait: 3 frame(s)
:              : $>Turn Up
:              : $>Through ON
@>Set Move Route: Player (Skip, Wait)
:              : $>1 Step Forward
@>Erase Event
@>
```

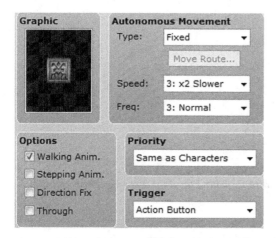

Figure 3-5. Details for page 2 of the door event

While the player does not possess the key, he/she will receive a description of the door. When the Catacomb Key is acquired, the player can open the door. This event is a tweaked version of the Quick Door Event present within RMVXA. Note that the door event has no Transfer Event. It is trivial to transfer the player beyond the wall to the other side of the level, but I do something a little different. Two wall tiles separate the player from the northern half of the catacombs once he/she has opened the door. We can use events with Above Characters priority to take on the appearance of wall tiles and let the player pass under them. How?

Creating Wall Tiles That the Player Can Pass Through

By creating wall tiles that allow the player to pass through them, we can (among other uses) create secret passages that remain unseen by players who are not so perceptive. In this case, we want to make it so that the player can pass through the doorway leading to the rest of the level. We can use wall tiles to the same effect. Here's how we can do that:

- Go to the Tilesets tab of the Database and find the Dungeon tileset in the list at the left part of the section.

- Once there, find **D:** in the Graphics section. Note how it is entirely blank. Click the "..." button and select the Dungeon_A4 tileset.

- With that done, you can now use wall tiles from the Dungeon tileset as event graphics.

- Next, find the spot where you want to place a wall tile. Right-click to create a new event. Use an identical graphic to that of the surrounding walls and give the event a Priority of Above Characters. Its Contents will be completely empty. See Figure 3-6 for a screenshot of the finished result.

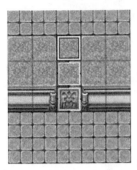

Figure 3-6. Wall tiles as event graphics directly behind the door event previously created

---

■ **Note** Make sure you place floor tiles beneath the event graphics! As some tiles in RMVXA are impassable, you want to make sure that the tiles under your special wall tile events are passable. An easy way to check if you have tiles beneath your graphic events is to switch to Region Mode, which renders all events temporarily invisible.

The Treasure Room

As noted near the start of the chapter, we have a treasure room on the map that contains four chests. If the player interacts with the small gap (Figure 3-7) in the northwestern wall of the catacombs, he/she will find the passage that leads to the treasure room.

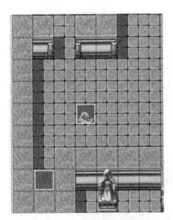

Figure 3-7. The passage event is located two spaces left and three spaces south of the slime

The event for the secret passage is two pages long.

Page 1 of 2
Priority: Same As Characters
Trigger: Action Button
```
@>Text: -, -, Normal, Bottom
:      : You have found a secret entrance!
@>Fadeout Screen
@>Transfer Player:[007:Level 1] (001,024), None
@>Control Self Switch: A =ON
@>Fadein Screen
@>
```

Page 2 of 2
Conditions: Self Switch A is ON
Priority: Same As Characters
Trigger: Action Button
```
@>Transfer Player:[007:Level 1] (001,024)
@>
```

This event has the following behavior:

- The first time players press the Action button while facing the secret passage event, they will receive a message notifying them that they have found a secret entrance.

- The screen will fade out and players will be transferred to the passage's exit near the four chests. *The None after the destination coordinates designates that Fade is turned off for that particular Transfer Event.*

- We flip a self-switch that is required by page 2 of this event.

- Finally, we use Fadein Screen to end the fade effect caused by Fadeout Screen.

- The second and subsequent times at which players interact with this event, they will be transferred immediately, without any of the extra lines used in page 1.

The graphic that will be used for the revealed passage (page 2 of this event) is one of the Entrance (Top Half) tiles in tab B of the Dungeon tileset. Figure 3-8 displays which tile we'll be using.

Figure 3-8. *The tile used for page 2's graphic is the third tile on the bottom row of this 3×3 group of entrances and exits. It is a black block*

When players locate the secret passage, they'll find themselves at the position indicated in Figure 3-9.

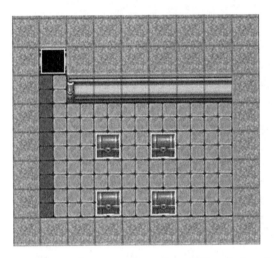

Figure 3-9. *The secret treasure room. Note the location of the event leading back to the rest of the level*

The event leading back to the rest of the level is the following.

Graphic: Entrance (Top Half)
Priority: Same As Characters
Trigger: Action Button
@>Transfer Player:[007:Level 1] (001,009)
@>

As for the contents of the chests themselves, this is where we can have some fun with the fact that there are three playable characters.

Creating Chests with Contents Dependent on Characters

It wouldn't do much good for Palnor to find a spell scroll. In the same way, Feylia (or Gust, for that matter) wouldn't be too happy to find a two-handed axe. To make a chest having differing contents dependent on the player's character, we can adapt the Quick Treasure Chest Event (accessible quickly by pressing Ctrl+3 after left-clicking the square on which you wish to add your event). If we were to use the Quick Treasure Chest Event to create a chest with 0 Gold (functionally empty), it would look like the following:

Page 1 of 2
Graphic: Closed red treasure chest in the upper-right corner of the !Chest graphic set.
Options: Direction Fix
Priority: Same as Characters
Trigger: Action Button
Contents:

```
@>Play SE: 'Chest', 80, 100
@>Set Move Route: This event (Wait)
:                  : $>Direction Fix OFF
:                  : $>Turn Left
:                  : $>Wait: 3 frame(s)
:                  : $>Turn Right
:                  : $>Wait: 3 frame(s)
@>Control Self Switch: A =ON
@>Change Gold: + 0
@>Text: -, -, Normal, Bottom
:       : 0\G were found!
@>
```

Page 2 of 2
Graphic: Open red treasure chest three tiles below the upper-right corner of the !Chest graphic set.
Condition: Self Switch A is ON
Options: Direction Fix
Priority: Same as Characters
Trigger: Action Button
No Contents

So, what we want to do is copy the first page two times. Then, each of the first three pages will have a character conditional. For example, page 1 will require that the Palnor switch be on, while page 2 will require the Gust switch to be on. Page 3, logically, would run if the Feylia switch were on. In that way, we can give each character the most appropriate treasure! For the sake of brevity, I will merely show what should change in each of the first three pages, based on what we want each character to retrieve from the chest. For this exercise, let's edit the upper-left treasure chest.

Page 1 of 4
Condition: Switch 0001: Palnor is ON
Replace **Change Gold: + 0** with **Change Weapons: [Bronze Greatsword] + 1**
@>Text: -, -, Normal, Bottom
: 　　: Received Bronze Greatsword!
Page 2 of 4
Condition: Switch 0002: Gust is ON
Replace **Change Gold: + 0** with **Change Weapons: [Bronze Bow] + 1**
@>Text: -, -, Normal, Bottom
: 　　: Received Bronze Bow!
Page 3 of 4
Condition: Switch 0001: Feylia is ON
Replace **Change Gold: + 0** with **Change Weapons: [Stone Staff] + 1**
@>Text: -, -, Normal, Bottom
: 　　: Received Stone Staff!

Split the following rewards among the three other treasure chests:

- Cloth Cap

- 200 Gold

- Studded Leather

With that said and done, the last thing left to do for Level 1 is to create a Parallel Process event that can cover the transfer events for the two staircases in the level. While we have yet to create Level 2, we can prepare the event beforehand, so that it only needs us to add the appropriate Transfer Player event command once we're ready. Without further ado, here's the relevant event that will cover the transfer events for both staircases:

Trigger: Parallel Process
@>Control Variables: [0019:X] = Player's Map X
@>Control Variables: [0020:Y] = Player's Map Y
@>Conditional Branch: Variable [0019:X] == 30
　@>Conditional Branch: Variable [0020:Y] == 1
　　@>
　: Branch End
　@>
: Branch End
@>Conditional Branch: Variable [0019:X] == 10
　@>Conditional Branch: Variable [0020:Y] == 23
　　@>Transfer Player:[001:Eagle's Crossing] (012,004), Down
　　@>
　: Branch End
　@>
: Branch End
@>

■ **Note**   The Priority setting of a Parallel Process is essentially pointless. The same is largely true of the Priority setting of Autorun events.

I like to place Parallel Process events in otherwise unreachable locations. That way, I can assure myself that the player cannot attempt to interact with them directly. It's not really necessary to do this, but that's how I do it. With that, I could say that we're done with the chapter, but I *do* have one very broad area left to cover.

Creating the Spell Scrolls

Much earlier in the chapter, I hinted that we would be creating spell scrolls from which Feylia and Gust could learn new spells. This particular exercise is too nuanced for bullets to do it justice. As you have seen in your time working with RMVXA (which I'll cover in greater detail in Chapter 4), Items have an Effects section that works much like Features do for Actors, Classes, and so forth. The Effect we're interested in is Learn Skill, which is located in the Others tab of the Effects dialog menu, as shown in Figure 3-10.

Figure 3-10. *The Others tab of the Effects dialog menu*

Considerations

You would think that creating a spell scroll would be as easy as selecting the skill you wish the scroll to impart and then pressing OK. You'd be wrong. Why? Well, what stops Palnor from reading any spell scroll, or Gust from reading scrolls holding spells he's not supposed to be able to learn? That's the main worry. There are two ways to work around those issues.

1. **Police where spell scrolls can be acquired**: All things considered, that shouldn't be too hard to do. Our game has three sources of item acquisition, and none of them is random.

   a. **Shops**: The player can acquire spell scrolls from the Magic Shop. We can use the same principle we apply to treasure chests: having dedicated pages (or conditional branches) for each of the characters. Palnor will receive little more than a few words of conversation, but Gust and Feylia will be able to buy spells (Feylia can also buy staves). So, we make it so that Gust can only buy spell scrolls for the spells he can learn and then give Feylia the entire inventory.

   b. **Enemy loot drops**: While neither the Rat nor the Slime drops any items, the same will not be true of enemies discussed in later chapters. Because we can't make loot drops discriminate among players, the best idea would be to make it so that enemies cannot drop scrolls.

   c. **Treasure Chests**: This is pretty much self-explanatory. All we have to do is make chests with contents that differ, based on the player opening them.

2. **Use common events to flesh out spell scroll behavior.**

The second method is the best way to go about this situation. The first method (of policing) will be pretty much impossible, when I introduce a certain thing in Chapter 4. There are a total of 18 spells in our game. This is how they break down:

- Palnor cannot learn any of the 18 spells. So, if he were to somehow acquire and use a scroll, it would return an error message and not be consumed.

- Gust can learn the first 6 spells in the game. If he somehow gets his hands on a scroll containing a spell in the latter 12, he should not be able to learn the spell that it contains.

- Feylia starts with the first 6 spells in the game and can learn the other 12 via spell scrolls whenever she gains access to them (either by finding one in a treasure chest or by buying it from the Magic Shop).

In every case, error messages should be returned if the player character cannot learn a spell (either because he/she is not allowed or because he/she already possesses knowledge of it). We can use the individual character switches for conditional branches, and we have established that there are two categories of spells.

Eventing the Spell Scrolls

So, here's the event code for LearnFire, the common event that governs the Scroll of Fire item (we'll create the item in the next page). Fire is a spell that Gust can learn but Feylia already possesses. Common events are a variant of events that can be used for (among other things) adding special effects to items. Make your way to the Common Events tab in the Database and use the following event code for the LearnFire common event:

```
Trigger: None
@>Conditional Branch: Switch [0001:Palnor] == ON
  @>Text: -, -, Normal, Bottom
  :     : You open the scroll, but can't make heads or tails
  :     : of what is written on it.
  @>
: Branch End
@>Conditional Branch: Switch [0002:Gust] == ON
  @>Conditional Branch: Gust is [Fire] Learned == ON
    @>Text: -, -, Normal, Bottom
    :     : You already know that spell!
    @>
   : Else
    @>Change Items: [Scroll of Fire], - 1
    @>Change Skills: [Gust], + [Fire]
    @>
  : Branch End
  @>
: Branch End
@>Conditional Branch: Switch [0003:Feylia] == ON
  @>Text: -, -, Normal, Bottom
  :     : You already know that spell!
  @>
: Branch End
@>
```

Of course, this common event is useless unless we actually create the Scroll of Fire item, so let's do that real quick. Head over to the Items tab and see Figure 3-11.

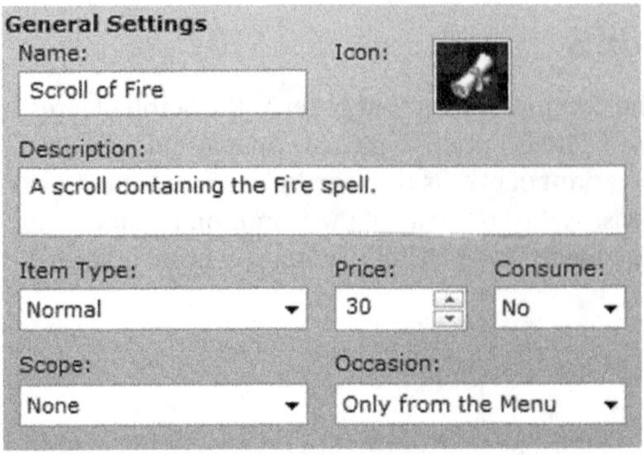

General Settings

Name: Scroll of Fire

Icon:

Description: A scroll containing the Fire spell.

Item Type: Normal

Price: 30

Consume: No

Scope: None

Occasion: Only from the Menu

Figure 3-11. General Settings for the Scroll of Fire item

Create that item in slot 15 of the Items tab and then copy it 17 times, to provide a scroll for each of our 18 spells. The only things that change between scrolls are their name, description, price, and called common event. Thus, it's far quicker just to copy and fix, rather than transcribe the same thing 18 times. You can also copy the LearnFire common event 5 times and make the appropriate changes for each new spell. As you can imagine, the Scroll of Fire calls the LearnFire common event (this is yet another possible item Effect) when used from the menu.

■ **Note** I organized the scrolls and their associated common events in the order that I display them in this chapter's tables. You should do the same, as it allows you to more easily separate the spells both Gust and Feylia can learn from those that only Feylia can learn.

Now, let's have a spell from the second category, that is, a spell that only Feylia may learn. This is the LearnBlaze common event.

```
Trigger: None
@>Conditional Branch: Switch [0003:Feylia] == OFF
  @>Text: -, -, Normal, Bottom
  :     : You open the scroll, but can't make heads or tails
  :     : of what is written on it.
  @>
: Branch End
@>Conditional Branch: Switch [0003:Feylia] == ON
  @>Conditional Branch: Feylia is [Blaze] Learned == ON
    @>Text: -, -, Normal, Bottom
    :     : You already know that spell!
    @>
```

```
  : Else
  @>Change Items: [Scroll of Blaze], - 1
  @>Change Skills: [Feylia], + [Blaze]
  @>
  : Branch End
  @>
: Branch End
```

A quick look at both of the common events shown here reveals both similarities and differences. In the first category of spells, we check to see if the player is playing as Palnor. If he/she is, then we return an error message when the scroll is used. If the player is playing as Gust, the game then checks to see if Gust has learned Fire. If he has, then the game will note the fact. Otherwise, a Scroll of Fire will be consumed, and Gust will learn Fire. Because Feylia starts with Fire, we can skip the check and return the "skill already known" error message. In the second category of spells, we only have to check to see if the player is *not* playing as Feylia—because neither Gust nor Palnor can learn these spells—and then return an error message if he/she isn't. If he/she is, we perform the same check we did for Gust in the first category of spells, to see, this time, if Feylia already knows the spell.

■ **Note**   This is probably the most appropriate time to finish up the 12 common events you'll have to match with Feylia's spell scrolls. It's good practice to go through and do this yourself or, if you're in a hurry, you can use the files from the book's download package.

Summary

During the course of this chapter, we created the upper half of the catacombs of Eagle's Crossing. We added monster encounters that move around the map; a simple level objective in the form of a key, which that the player requires to complete progress; and a secret treasure room that rewards the player for exploring his/her surroundings in great detail. We even tackled the issue of teaching spells to our player characters. In the next chapter, we will complete Eagle's Crossing.

CHAPTER 4

■ ■ ■

Populating Eagle's Crossing

While a part of the very first chapter of this book was dedicated to creating the various locations within Eagle's Crossing, now's the perfect time to populate the town's shops and add nonplayer characters (NPCs), as needed. I opted to reserve doing this until the fourth chapter and not the third, because it mirrors my personal dungeon crawler play style: rush right into the dungeon and then return to town, as low HP or an excess of loot demands. So, how am I going to go about this? There are four buildings, so let's tackle them in clockwise fashion, starting from the Equipment Shop in the upper-left corner.

Populating the Equipment Shop

In this section, we'll flesh out the two NPCs that will be running the Equipment Shop. Recall from Chapter 1 that our NPCs are graphics, with no event contents to speak of. Before we begin, it would be good to take two things into consideration.

- **Do I want the player to be able to see the entire shop inventory from the start of the game?** In most role-playing games (RPGs), our dungeon crawler included, the actual deterrent to being able to get the best equipment from the start of the game isn't availability but, rather, currency. So, it doesn't matter whether we show off everything that the player can buy. If anything, it could provide a degree of impetus for him/her to want to begin dungeon crawling, to be able to buy the better stuff.

- **Do I show off the whole shop inventory for all characters?** I'm inclined to answer this with a no. Take the Weapon Shop, for example. There's no point in Gust seeing two-handed weapons that he cannot use. Feylia is an extreme case and should only see daggers (we'll be selling the four staff weapons at the Magic Shop). Palnor wouldn't want to see bows that he cannot use either.

On that note, here's the event for the Weapon Shop NPC.

■ **Note** Unless strictly necessary, I won't mention the graphics for NPCs in my event code. Feel free to use the Character Generator to make your own fresh faces. Alternately, if you'd rather go stock, I'm quite partial to the People1 and People2 graphic sets for shop NPCs They contain quite a few sprites that could conceivably be shopkeepers and/or merchants.

```
Priority: Same as Characters
Trigger: Action Button
@>Text: -, -, Normal, Bottom
:       : Welcome to the weapon shop!
:       : What can I do for you?
@>Conditional Branch: Switch [0001:Palnor] == ON
  @>Shop Processing: [Wooden Axe]
  :                : [Wooden Greataxe]
  :                : [Wooden Dagger]
  :                : [Wooden Sword]
  :                : [Wooden Greatsword]
  @>
: Branch End
@>Conditional Branch: Switch [0002:Gust] == ON
  @>Shop Processing: [Wooden Axe]
  :                : [Wooden Arrow]
  :                : [Wooden Bow]
  :                : [Wooden Dagger]
  :                : [Wooden Sword]
  @>
: Branch End
@>Conditional Branch: Switch [0003:Feylia] == ON
  @>Shop Processing: [Wooden Dagger]
  @>
: Branch End
@>
```

For space considerations, I used only weapons of the Wooden tier to show what each character would see in the Weapon Shop. It shouldn't take you more than a few minutes to fill out each character's Weapon Shop inventory, despite the fact that both Palnor and Gust have a whopping 30 (!) possible weapons.

■ **Note** If you can't stand the sight of so many items on the same shopping list, you could use Show Choices to split the inventory into more manageable chunks. See the following code for a sample event.

```
@>Show Choices: Wood and Copper, Bronze and Iron, Steel and Mythril, Leave
: When [Wood and Copper]
  @>Comment: Insert relevant weapons in this shop.
  @>
: When [Bronze and Iron]
  @>Comment: Insert relevant weapons in this shop.
  @>
: When [Steel and Mythril]
  @>Comment: Insert relevant weapons in this shop.
  @>
: When [Leave]
  @>
: Branch End
@>
```

I used a comment in place of a Shop Processing event command for the sake of saving space. The Armor Shop works in much the same way, so I'll skip elaborating on it entirely. You can just copy the Weapon Shop NPC event contents and change the Shop Processing contents appropriately. Just remember that Feylia can only use Light Armor, Gust can use Light Armor and Medium Armor, and Palnor can use any type of armor.

Populating the Pub

Tavern, pub, inn. No matter which of the three names the given locale has in a game, they all have the same purpose: to serve as a place for the player character to recover from battle wounds. The pub of Eagle's Crossing allows players to rest (free of charge) and even recruit a companion to aid them in their quest for the sacred artifact. See Figure 4-1 of how the Pub should look after you are done with this section.

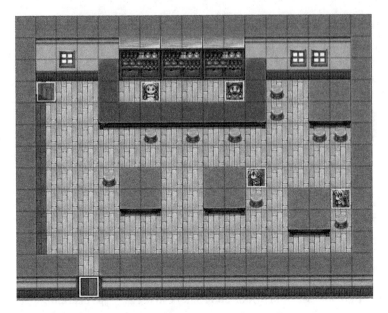

Figure 4-1. *The completed Pub*

There are six events in the pub. I'll list them in order of importance, from most to least (relatively speaking, of course).

- The two NPCs sitting at the Pub's tables will serve as potential companions for the player.

- The NPC at the right side of the counter will alert the player to potential companions, if he/she does not yet have one. If the player does have a companion, the NPC will allow the player to dismiss them, upon which they will return to their tables.

- The NPC at the left side of the counter is the innkeeper. She allows the player to rest, restoring their character's HP and MP completely free of charge.

- There is a transfer event placed one square below the entrance to the Pub. If you didn't add this back in Chapter 1, now would be the time to do so.

- Last, the stairs trigger an event when stepped on, prompting the player to speak to the innkeeper, if he/she wishes to rest.

Creating Our Companions

We can create our game's pair of companions in much the same way we made our three main characters. First, let's create the new classes for our would-be companions. If you need a refresher, you'll want to go back to Chapter 2 and reread what was covered in the "Overview" section of that chapter. When you're ready to move on, please see Table 4-1.

Table 4-1. *Base Stats, Stat Growths, and Theoretical Maximum Stats of the Fighter and Apprentice Companion Classes*

Class	MHP	MMP	ATK	DEF	MAT	MDF	AGI	LUK
Fighter (basestats)	40	0	2	2	1	1	1	1
Fighter (stats per level)	4	0	0.75	0.75	0	0.25	0.5	0.5
Fighter (max stats at Level 99)	432	0	76	76	1	25	50	50
Apprentice (base stats)	20	20	1	1	2	2	1	1
Apprentice (stats per level)	2	2	0.25	0.25	0.75	0.5	0.5	0.5
Apprentice (max stats at Level 99)	216	314	25	25	76	51	50	50

If the preceding classes and their growths seem derivative of our existent classes, that's because they are. The Fighter is basically a toned-down version of the Warrior, while the Apprentice is, likewise, a weaker version of the Mage, with most of the features of their respective "parent" classes. Speaking of features, please take a look at Table 4-2.

Table 4-2. *Features List of the Fighter and Apprentice Companion Classes*

Class Name	HIT%	CRI%	Equip Weapon	Equip Armor	Add Skill Type
Fighter	80	5	Axe, Dagger, Sword	Light Armor, Medium Armor	No
Apprentice	70	5	Dagger, Staff	Light Armor	Magic

■ **Note** The Apprentice starts with the same spells that Feylia does but cannot learn new spells via spell scrolls.

The two companions, while not as strong or able as the player character, are both worthy allies when the going gets tough. Go to the Classes tab and create them in the same way you created the first three classes in Chapter 2. Afterward, go to the Actors tab and give both of the player's potential companions appropriate graphics and starting equipment. See Figure 4-2.

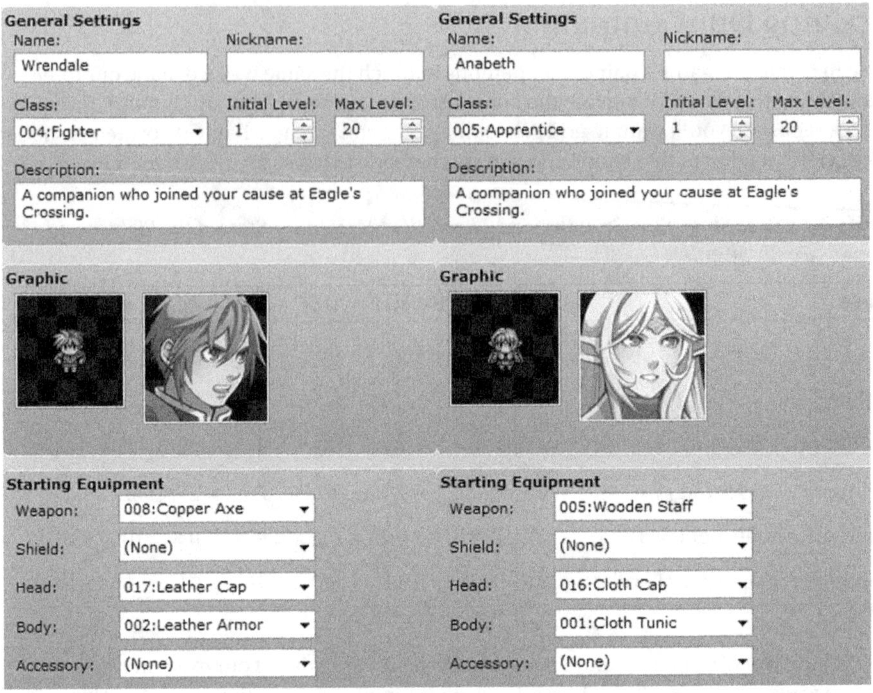

Figure 4-2. *The Actors tab entries for Wrendale the Fighter and Anabeth the Apprentice*

Eventing Our Companions

With that out of the way, we can get started with eventing the logic concerning our companions. Keep in mind that the player will only be able to have one companion with him/her at a time. Both of the companions use a similar two-page event that covers the following behavior:

- If the player has no companions, the pair will offer their services to him/her. Saying "no" does nothing, but saying "yes" adds the two to the player's party, removing their sprites from the Pub.

- If the player has already recruited one of the companions, the two will point out the fact and ask the player to return once he/she has dismissed his/her companion.

■ **Note** Before starting this section in earnest, take a moment to go to the System tab of the Database and uncheck the Show Player Followers check box. While being able to see your full party on the screen is cool, this is also subject to collision detection and could interfere with events. I feel it is better to keep it nice and simple with the single visible character.

In any case, here is the event code for Wrendale the Fighter:

Page 1 of 2
Graphic: Second left-facing sprite in the upper-left section of Actor1
Priority: Same as Characters
Contents
```
@>Conditional Branch: Switch [0004: Companion] == ON
  @>Text: 'Actor1', 0, Normal, Bottom
  :      : I see you already have company. Call me
  :      : up if you need me.
  @>
: Branch End
@>Conditional Branch: Switch [0004: Companion] == OFF
  @>Text: 'Actor1', 0, Normal, Bottom
  :      : Hail, adventurer. My name is Wrendale.
  :      : I have come to Eagle's Crossing in
  :      : search of glory. Will you allow me to
  :      : quest with you?
  @>Show Choices: Yes, No
  : When [Yes]
    @>Text: 'Actor1', 0, Normal, Bottom
    :      : My thanks! Let us be off!
    @>Fadeout Screen
    @>Text: -, -, Normal, Bottom
    :      : Wrendale has joined your party!
    @>Change Party Member: Add [Wrendale]
    @>Control Switches: [0004:Companion] = ON
    @>Control Switches: [0005:Wrendale] = ON
    @>Fadein Screen
    @>
  : When [No]
    @>Text: 'Actor1', 0, Normal, Bottom
    :      : I will await your return!
    @>
  : Branch End
  @>
: Branch End
@>
```
Page 2 of 2
Graphic: None
Priority: Below Characters
Condition: Switch 0005:Wrendale is ON
No Contents

You can copy this same event for Anabeth the Apprentice. Her sprite set is the second one (of four) in the lower row of Actor3. Because Anabeth isn't as concerned with fame or glory, you can replace Wrendale's greetings with: Greetings. My name is Anabeth. I have come to Eagle's Crossing in search of knowledge. Will you allow me to quest with you?

■ **Tip**   You can use the Preview button in the Show Text command to ensure that your lines are set up correctly and are not stretching beyond the visible part of the text box.

Besides that, just tweak the event, as required, and use a different switch (since Wrendale was switch 0005, Anabeth will be switch 0006) for Anabeth, and you're set!

Creating the Dismissal NPC

Having a companion is all well and good, but what if the player wanted to switch? You could create an item with a common event that allows the player to swap characters, but let's keep things simple. Let's create an NPC that handles the dismissal of the player's current companion, so that he/she can hire the other one. Here's the event code for the NPC:

Page 1 of 2
Priority: Same as Characters
Trigger: Action Button
@>Text: -, -, Normal, Bottom
:   : Hello, adventurer. If you need a companion to
:   : assist you in your quest, two other adventurers
:   : arrived here recently. They're sitting at the tables
:   : there yonder.

Page 2 of 2
Condition: Switch 0004:Companion is ON
Priority: Same as Characters
Trigger: Action Button
@>Text: -, -, Normal, Bottom
:   : Hello there, adventurer. I see you have a companion
:   : with you already. Would you like to dismiss them?
@>Show Choices: Yes, No
: When [Yes]
  @>Conditional Branch: [Wrendale] is in the Party
    @>Text: 'Actor1', 0, Normal, Bottom
    :   : I take my leave.
    @>Change Party Member: Remove [Wrendale]
    @>Fadeout Screen
    @>Control Switches: [0004:Companion] = OFF

```
  @>Control Switches: [0005:Wrendale] = OFF
  @>Wait: 60 frame(s)
  @>Fadein Screen
  @>
 : Branch End
 @>Conditional Branch: [Anabeth] is in the Party
  @>Text: 'Actor3', 5, Normal, Bottom
   :     : I take my leave.
  @>Change Party Member: Remove [Anabeth]
  @>Fadeout Screen
  @>Control Switches: [0004:Companion] = OFF
  @>Control Switches: [0006:Anabeth] = OFF
  @>Wait: 60 frame(s)
  @>Fadein Screen
  @>
 : Branch End
 @>
: When [No]
 @>Text: -, -, Normal, Bottom
 :      : Fare thee well.
 @>
: Branch End
@>
```

Not much to say about this NPC. If the player has no companion, he/she will speak of the two adventurers who arrived at Eagle's Crossing recently. If he/she does have a companion, he/she can speak with the NPC to dismiss the companion. The companion will then sit back down at his or her starting position at the inn, waiting for the next time that he/she can aid the player in his/her quest.

■ **Note** Keep in mind that having an extra party member will affect your game's balance. Everything is easier when you have two characters instead of one. I'll be taking the companion's presence into account, starting from Chapter 6. In other words, once the player finds him-/herself in the Caves, they're probably going to want the extra help.

With that done, we can call this section concluded. The next section will tackle completing the events for the town buildings. (Remember that we created the NPCs back in Chapter 1 but left them as little more than graphics, without any event commands governing them.)

Creating the Innkeeper NPC

Thanks to the Inn Quick Event in RMVXA, this action barely merits a section. What I am going to do here is use the Quick Event to create an inn that costs no gold to rest at and then polish the event so that it doesn't read weird. See, the innkeeper's first Show Text event command announces the price of the inn and asks if the player wants to rest. It's a little silly for anyone to say: "It costs 0 G to rest here...." Besides, it will make the event shorter and neater. Take a look at the code to see the polished result.

```
Priority: Same as Characters
Trigger: Action Button
@>Text: -, -, Normal, Bottom
:      : This inn is free for adventurers.
:      : Would you like to stay?
@>Show Choices: Yes, No
: When [Yes]
  @>Fadeout Screen
  @>Play ME: 'Inn', 100, 100
  @>Wait: 300 frame(s)
  @>Recover All: Entire Party
  @>Fadein Screen
  @>
: When [No]
  @>Text: -, -, Normal, Bottom
  :      : Fare thee well.
  @>
: Branch End
@>
```

Looks a lot neater, if I do say so myself. That leaves the transfer event and the staircase event. First, let's create the transfer event. Right-click the square at 003,012, create a new event, and add the following event code to the newly created event.

```
Trigger: Player Touch
@>Play SE: 'Move', 80, 100
@>Transfer Player:[001:Eagle's Crossing] (018,011)
@>
```

■ **Note** Alternatively, you could use the Quick Transfer Event option to create the transfer event as well. As a reminder, you can find quick events for doors, chests, transfer events, and inns via the menu that opens when you right-click a square in Event Editing Mode.

Given that we have no actual second floor map for our game's Pub, we should at least have an event concerning the staircase. This is a rather brief text event that tells the player to go talk to the innkeeper if he/she wishes to rest.

Priority: Below Characters
Trigger: Player Touch
```
@>Text: -, -, Normal, Bottom
:        : You hear the innkeeper call to you.
@>Text: -, -, Normal, Bottom
:        : If you wish to take a rest, please talk to me.
@>Set Move Route: Player (Wait)
:                   : $>Turn 180
:                   : $>1 Step Forward
@>
```

With that, we're done with the Pub. Next, we will visit the Magic Shop, where Feylia will make most of her purchases.

Populating the Magic Shop

The Magic Shop is host to a single, enigmatic NPC that sells spell scrolls and (in Feylia's case) staves. You can see the Magic Shop NPC event code below:

```
@>Text: -, -, Normal, Bottom
:        : Welcome to the Magic Shop!
@>Conditional Branch: Switch [0001:Palnor] == ON
  @>Text: -, -, Normal, Bottom
  :        : I'm afraid that you'll find little point to this
  :        : establishment. I do thank you for visiting.
  @>
: Branch End
@>Conditional Branch: Switch [0002:Gust] == ON
  @>Text: -, -, Normal, Bottom
  :        : I see you have some knack for magicks arcana.
  :        : Here is what I can offer you.
  @>Shop Processing: [Scroll of Fire]
  :                   : [Scroll of Ice]
  :                   : [Scroll of Lesser Heal]
  :                   : [Scroll of Purge]
  :                   : [Scroll of Return]
  :                   : [Scroll of Shock]
  @>
: Branch End
```

```
@>Conditional Branch: Switch [0003:Feylia] == ON
  @>Text: -, -, Normal, Bottom
  :       : An honor to meet with such a scion of magical
  :       : prowess! Here's what I have available!
  @>Shop Processing: [Wooden Staff]
  :                : [Stone Staff]
  :                : [Obsidian Staff]
  :                : [Crystal Staff]
  :                : [Scroll of Blaze]
  :                : [Scroll of Bolt]
  :                : [Scroll of Chill]
  :                : [Scroll of Heal]
  :                : [Scroll of Sleep]
  :                : [Scroll of Blizzard]
  :                : [Scroll of Cleanse]
  :                : [Scroll of Greater Heal]
  :                : [Scroll of Immolate]
  :                : [Scroll of Poison Cloud]
  :                : [Scroll of Sleep Wave]
  :                : [Scroll of Thunder Storm]
  @>
: Branch End
@>
```

In the preceding event, if Palnor visits the Magic Shop, the NPC will note that there's not much point to him being there. If Gust or Feylia visits, he will bring appropriate wares for the respective characters. Not much else to say about this one. Create the appropriate transfer event for this area. (You can copy the transfer event we used for the Pub, but don't forget to change the destination!) Now let's move on to the last of Eagle's Crossing locales.

Populating the Item Shop

You may recall from Chapter 1 that we did not make an interior for the Item Shop. Unlike the other shops, we can have a single unified inventory for both Gust and Feylia. In Palnor's case, we could consider having a more abbreviated inventory. As we haven't covered what consumable items will exist in our game (with the sole exception of the first two potions), Table 4-3 will provide the needed information.

Table 4-3. *A List of All Consumable Items in Our Game*

Item Name	Description	Cost
Lesser Healing Potion	Heals 35 HP	10 G
Lesser Magic Potion	Heals 30 MP	20 G
Lesser Restoration Potion	Heals 35 HP and 30 MP	50 G
Return Crystal	Returns the party to town	50 G
Healing Potion	Heals 110 HP	50 G
Magic Potion	Heals 70 MP	100 G
Restoration Potion	Heals 110 HP and 70 MP	250 G
Antidote	Removes Poison from an ally	10 G
Smelling Salts	Awakens a sleeping ally	10 G
Para-Cure	Removes Paralysis from an ally	20 G
Voice Box	Removes Silence from an ally	15 G
Eye Drops	Removes Blindness from an ally	15 G
Panacea	Cures an ally of all negative status effects	50 G
Phoenix Tears	An extremely rare draught that can revive an ally at 50% HP	250 G

■ **Note** An item that is used on a dead ally has to have a scope of One Ally (Dead). Similarly, an item that is used on all dead allies should have a scope of All Allies (Dead). Failing to change the scope appropriately will render your revival item useless.

As you can see, our game has 14 consumable items that will be available for sale at the Item Shop. Palnor's inventory should probably not have items that restore MP (if you decide to split the inventories, depending on the active player character). In that case, he will be able to buy 9 of the items. Edit the event we created in Chapter 1 and add a relevant Shop Processing event command that allows the Item Shop to sell the above items to the player. You can find the completed version of this event in the source code download for this book.

Companions and Shops

Now, then, what happens if we want our companion to buy equipment from the Equipment Shop? Our events for our shops only take into account the player character. This is all well and good if Wrendale is hired with Palnor or Gust or Anabeth is hired with Feylia. But what happens if the player hires Wrendale with Feylia, for example? The player will only be able to buy daggers and light armor, although he/she is more than capable of using other weapons and armor. So, how do we remedy this? The easiest way is to add a second page that requires that Companion be set to ON. Here's what the Weapon Shop event could look like.

```
@>Text: -, -, Normal, Bottom
:      : Welcome to the weapon shop! I see that you have
:      : a companion with you. Who will shop today?
@>Show Choices: Me, My Companion, Nevermind
: When [Me]
  @>Conditional Branch: [0001:Palnor] == ON
    @>Shop Processing: (insert relevant items here)
    @>
  : Branch End
  @>Conditional Branch: [0002:Gust] == ON
    @>Shop Processing: (insert relevant items here)
    @>
  : Branch End
  @>Conditional Branch: [0003:Feylia] == ON
    @>Shop Processing: (insert relevant items here)
    @>
  : Branch End
  @>
: When [My Companion]
  @>Conditional Branch: [0005:Wrendale] == ON
    @>Shop Processing: (insert one-handed axes/swords and daggers here)
    @>
  : Branch End
  @>Conditional Branch: [0006:Anabeth] == ON
    @>Shop Processing: (insert daggers here)
    @>
  : Branch End
  @>
: When [Nevermind]
  @>
: Branch End
@>
```

■ **Tip**   To save some time when adding the companion's shop inventories, keep in mind that Wrendale and Gust share the same weapon permissions, save for bows, while Anabeth and Feylia have identical weapon permissions. For armor, Wrendale and Anabeth share the same permissions as Gust and Feylia, respectively.

The Magic Shop is even easier, as Anabeth cannot learn new spells, and Wrendale has no use for the shop, much like Palnor. When Anabeth is in the party, she only has to have access to the four different types of staves. Now, let's discuss the Return Crystal.

Creating the Return Item

Every other item in Table 4-3 should be easy to add to the Database. However, the Return Crystal requires a little more work. As promised in the previous chapter, we are going to discuss how to create an effect that allows the player to return to town from the dungeon. Essentially, you'll need a common event to handle logic and the item/skill to hold the common event (of which we have both an item and a skill). In practice, you'll want two different common events (one for the spell version of Return and one for the item version). In its simplest form, you can create a Return event with a single line of code, like so:

```
@>Transfer Player:[001:Eagle's Crossing] (012,013), Down
```

However, that brings a rather important problem: **A total lack of error checking**. Is the player already in town? He/She will still be able to use the item/skill, which is a waste of resources. So, we should have a switch (I call it InTown) that is on when the player is within Eagle's Crossing and off when he/she is in the dungeon. Then, we can use conditional branches to cover both possibilities. For the item version of Return, you'll want to make sure the item in question has Consume set to No. Then, you can use a Change Items event command to reduce the number of Return Crystals by 1 when it is successfully used. Basically, what we're doing here is shifting the Consume property from the actual item to its associated event. For the item event, the player is asked whether he/she wishes to return to town and given a yes/no option. We only want the player to lose a Return Crystal when he/she chooses yes. For the spell event, the player is instantly returned to town.

```
Name: ReturnItem
Trigger: None
@>Conditional Branch: Switch [0009:InTown] == ON
  @>Text: -, -, Normal, Bottom
  :     : You're already in town!
  @>
: Branch End
```

```
@>Conditional Branch: Switch [0009:InTown] == OFF
  @>Text: -, -, Normal, Bottom
  :      : Would you like to return to town?
  @>Show Choices: Yes, No
  : When [Yes]
    @>Control Switches: [0009:InTown] = ON
    @>Change Items: [Return Crystal], -1
    @>Play SE: 'Teleport', 80, 100
    @>Transfer Player:[001:Eagle's Crossing] (012,013), Down
    @>
  : When [No]
    @>
  : Branch End
  @>
: Branch End
@>


Name: ReturnSpell
Trigger: None
@>Conditional Branch: Switch [0009:InTown] == ON
  @>Text: -, -, Normal, Bottom
  :      : You're already in town!
  @>
: Branch End
@>Conditional Branch: Switch [0009:InTown] == OFF
  @>Control Switches: [0009:InTown] = ON
  @>Play SE: 'Teleport', 80, 100
  @>Transfer Player:[001:Eagle's Crossing] (012,013), Down
  @>
: Branch End
@>
```

Creating a Return Portal

So, as cool as the Return event is, it still has some room for improvement. What if we want our Return effect to create a portal in town that the player can use to quickly pop back to his/her previous location in the dungeon? To accomplish that, we'll have to add a portal event to Eagle's Crossing and declare a few new variables and switches. We'll place the portal event right in the middle of Eagle's Crossing (precisely where the player arrives via the Return spell, as a matter of fact). Here's the portal event code:

Condition: Switch 0007: Return is ON
Graphic: Ninth sprite on the final row of !Flame (Figure 4-3)

Figure 4-3. *Screenshot of the final row of !Flame*

Priority: Below Characters
Trigger: Action Button
Toggle Direction Fix

```
@>Text: -, -, Normal, Bottom
:      : Would you like to return to the dungeon?
@>Show Choices: Yes, No
: When [Yes]
  @>Control Switches: [0007:Return] = OFF
  @>Control Switches: [0009:InTown] = OFF
  @>Transfer Player: Variable [0015][0016][0017]
  @>
: When [No]
  @>
: Branch End
@>
```

The preceding code requires some explanation. First, we'll have a new switch called Return that flips on when the player uses a Return Crystal or the Return spell. When that switch is on, a portal appears in the middle of Eagle's Crossing. The player can interact with the portal by standing directly on it and pressing the Action button. The game will ask the player if he/she wishes to return to the dungeon. A *yes* will toggle off the Return and InTown switches and transfer the player to their previous location in the dungeon. Because the player can use a Return effect anywhere inside of the dungeon, we have to know exactly from where the player returned. For this, we use the **Designation with variables** option within the Transfer Player event command. To use that option, we have to create two new variables to hold another pair of x and y coordinates and a third to hold the dungeon map ID. Then, we have to expand our Return common events to account for this functionality. Given that the ReturnSpell event is shorter, I will be using that one. However, the same principles apply for ReturnItem as well. Look at the following to see ReturnSpell in its tweaked form.

Name: ReturnSpell

```
@>Conditional Branch: Switch [0009:InTown] == ON
  @>Text: -, -, Normal, Bottom
  :      : You're already in town!
  @>
: Branch End
@>Conditional Branch: Switch [0009:InTown] == OFF
  @>Control Variables: [0015:ReturnMapID] = Map ID
  @>Control Variables: [0016:ReturnX] = Player's Map X
  @>Control Variables: [0017:ReturnY] = Player's Map Y
  @>Control Switches: [0007:Return] = ON
  @>Control Switches: [0009:InTown] = ON
  @>Play SE: 'Teleport', 80, 100
  @>Transfer Player:[001:Eagle's Crossing] (012,013), Down
  @>
: Branch End
@>
```

■ **Note** You'll need to set InTown to on in the initial Autorun event that is triggered when the player is transferred from the character select map to Eagle's Crossing. This prevents a niche bug whereby the player can use Return (to essentially nil effect) to town before heading down to the dungeon for the first time.

Connecting Eagle's Crossing to the Upper Catacombs

For all of the work we've already done concerning this game's town, we still have to connect it with the first level of our dungeon. Let's get right on that. The following event code may look largely familiar.

```
Condition: Self Switch A is ON
Trigger: Parallel Process
@>Control Variables: [0019:X] = Player's Map X
@>Control Variables: [0020:Y] = Player's Map Y
@>Conditional Branch: Variable [0020:Y] == 3
  @>Conditional Branch: Self Switch B == OFF
    @>Control Variables: [0001:DeepestDungeonFloor] = 1
    @>Control Self Switch: B =ON
    @>Control Switches: [0009:InTown] = OFF
    @>Transfer Player:[007:Level 1] (010,022)
    @>
  : Else
    @>Control Switches: [0009:InTown] = OFF
    @>Transfer Player:[007:Level 1] (010,022)
    @>
  : Branch End
  @>
: Branch End
@>Conditional Branch: Variable [0019:X] == 6
  @>Conditional Branch: Variable [0020:Y] == 10
    @>Transfer Player:[002:Weapon Shop] (004,011), Up
    @>
  : Branch End
  @>
: Branch End
@>Conditional Branch: Variable [0019:X] == 18
  @>Conditional Branch: Variable [0020:Y] == 10
    @>Transfer Player:[003:Pub] (003,011), Up
    @>
  : Branch End
  @>
: Branch End
```

```
@>Conditional Branch: Variable [0019:X] == 18
  @>Conditional Branch: Variable [0020:Y] == 19
    @>Transfer Player:[004:Magic Shop] (007,011), Up
    @>
  : Branch End
  @>
: Branch End
@>
```

Of particular note (mostly because it's new code) is the transfer event that allows the player to enter the dungeon. If it is the first time that the player triggers that transfer event, the value of DeepestDungeonFloor will be set to 1, and the player will be sent to the dungeon. Storing how far the player has progressed can be useful, if you want shopkeepers to reveal their inventory gradually, or you want NPCs to talk about relevant events. For instance, take a look at the next section.

The Town Greeter

It's a dull job, but somebody has to do it. Who else but the town greeter can steer newly arrived visitors in the right direction? He stands stoically at 13,11 (one square northeast of the Return portal's event), waiting for player characters to speak with him. At the start of the game, he will give the player an overview of the town. As the player progresses, he will speak about rumors and other such miscellanea. Each time the player reaches a new level of the dungeon, the town greeter will have something new to say. Here are the first two pages of this NPC event, which covers the initial meeting and words spoken when the player has been to the first level.

Page 1 of 2
Priority: Same as Characters
Trigger: Action Button
Contents
```
@>Text: -, -, Normal, Bottom
:     : Welcome to Eagle's Crossing! I can see you're new
:     : here. Would you like me to talk about the town?
@>Show Choices: Yes, No
: When [Yes]
  @>Text: -, -, Normal, Bottom
  :     : We are in the Adventurer's Quarter of Eagle's
  :     : Crossing. This part of town was specifically
  :     : built a few years back for people such as yourself.
  :     : It provides most of the amenities of our fine town
  @>Text: -, -, Normal, Bottom
  :     : within walking distance. The upper-left building
  :     : sells weapons and armors. The upper right is the
  :     : pub, where you can recuperate from your trips to
  :     : the dungeon. The lower-right building is the magic
```

```
@>Text: -, -, Normal, Bottom
  :     : shop, where spell scrolls and staves can be
  :     : acquired. Last, the lower-left building is the
  :     : item shop, which sells curatives among other things.
  @>
: When [No]
  @>Text: -, -, Normal, Bottom
  :     : Very well.
  @>
: Branch End
@>Text: -, -, Normal, Bottom
  :     : Feel free to come talk to me every so often. I might
  :     : have something new or interesting to say, depending
  :     : on your progress in the dungeon.
@>Show Balloon Icon: This event, Music Note, Wait
@>
```

Page 2 of 2
Condition: 0001:DeepestDungeonFloor is 1 or above
Priority: Same as Characters
Trigger: Action Button
Contents

```
@>Text: -, -, Normal, Bottom
  :     : I see you've taken your first steps into the
  :     : dungeon. Vermin have made their home there.
  :     : It's been far too long since someone went in there
  :     : to do clean up. I thank you for your efforts.
```

Did the town greeter just break the fourth wall? Why, yes, he did. He's good at that, as you'll see in the course of the rest of the book. With that said and done, this chapter has reached its conclusion.

Summary

During the course of this chapter, we finished tweaking Eagle's Crossing and connected it with the dungeon's first level. In addition, we created two companions for the player's character and a way for the player to return to town instantly from the dungeon. In the next chapter, we will create the second level of our game's dungeon.

CHAPTER 5

■ ■ ■

The Lower Catacombs of Eagle's Crossing

In this chapter, we will be working on our dungeon's second level, the Lower Catacombs. A puzzle and stronger enemies will do their best to obstruct our player's progress.

The Lower Catacombs

The Lower Catacombs contain tombs and effigies of the most illustrious individuals of the world. Rumors speak of statues that come to life when their masters or their belongings are threatened...

If the player has cleared out the Upper Catacombs in their entirety, the experience gained should be just enough to push his/her character to Level 3.

■ **Note** It's generally a good idea to balance your monsters in later dungeon levels based on party size and experience levels.

Thus, it stands to reason that the enemies that the player will face in the Lower Catacombs should be stronger as well. Here's a list of things that I will be covering in this chapter.

- Making static encounters with a chance of having a single enemy or a pair of enemies.

- Making a very strong encounter that starts moving when the player tries to open one of the chests in the central tomb.

- Creating a puzzle that, when solved, allows the player to enter the central tomb.

- Following from the preceding, we must have several stone slabs that give the player hints as to how to solve the puzzle.

What Does the Town Greeter Have to Say?

From now to Chapter 9, every chapter will include this brief section. Basically, I'll write in it what the town greeter has to say about the area in question. This particular blurb requires that the DeepestDungeonVariable be set to 2. You can reference the second event page of our town greeter nonplayer character (NPC; detailed in the previous chapter) to create the following:

> *You made it to the Lower Catacombs, or so I've heard. There are four statues that have been there since the day my ancestors created the tombs. Mind yourself around them.*

Level Overview

The first order of business is to create the map itself. We will use the Dungeon tileset once again, with the same battleback (Cobblestones1 and Stone1) and BGM (Dungeon1) as the first level, and a map size of 59×47. See Figure 5-1 for a screenshot of the level in its entirety.

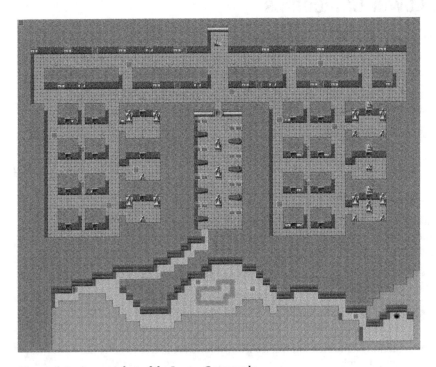

Figure 5-1. *A screenshot of the Lower Catacombs*

■ **Note**   You're going to notice from here on that my maps will all have a height of 47. That's the maximum map height, if you want your map to appear on a single screen in 1/2 scale, assuming your screen resolution is 1440×900. In any case, the maximum visible area (width and height) of a map in RPG Maker is dependent on your monitor's resolution. So, the higher the resolution, the more map tiles you will be able to see. I do it for the sake of the screenshots.

As with the level screenshot in Chapter 3, I have used an alternate wall tile to better contrast the otherwise gray catacomb walls in black-and-white renditions of this book. You can refer to the finished map in the source code download, to see what the map actually looks like.

Notable points of interest include the following:

- The hole in the lower-right corner of the area that leads down to the next level (the Caves).

- The smaller tombs on either side of the central tombs. The statues are key to figuring out the level's puzzle.

- The central tomb itself. Its entrance is barred by a gate that requires the player to correctly figure out the solution to its puzzle. Inside, there are a whopping 16 chests, of which only 7 contain anything. Opening any of them causes the strong enemy encounter to activate.

- The stone slabs near the staircase up to the Upper Catacombs. These hold hints to aid the player in figuring out the level's puzzle.

- The cave terrain in the lower half of the level. The walls use the Wall (Dirt Cave) tile, while the floor uses the Ground (Dirt Cave) tile.

Take some time to draw up the map or load it from the source code download package. Once the map is ready, move on to the next section.

Creating Transfer Events for the Upper Catacombs

Upper Catacombs? That may be the question you are asking yourself right now. After all, are we not in the Lower Catacombs? Well, given the way that I have broken down the dungeon chapters, it is more efficient for me to create the transfer events for the previous level while discussing the next level (basically because, otherwise, the lower level wouldn't exist for purposes of the staircase leading down).

There are two staircases in the first level of our game. The staircase leading down is at 030,001, while the staircase leading to town is at 010,023. You'll want to place a Parallel Process event somewhere in the Upper Catacombs, to cover these individual instances. As is usual, I prefer an otherwise inaccessible location for my Parallel Process events. Here's the event code in question:

```
Trigger: Parallel Process
@>Control Variables: [0019:X] = Player's Map X
@>Control Variables: [0020:Y] = Player's Map Y
@>Conditional Branch: Variable [0019:X] == 30
  @>Conditional Branch: Variable [0020:Y] == 1
    @>Conditional Branch: Self Switch B == OFF
      @>Control Variables: [0001:DeepestDungeonFloor] = 2
      @>Control Self Switch: B =ON
      @>Transfer Player:[008:Level 2] (029,004), Down
    : Else
      @>Transfer Player:[008:Level 2] (029,004), Down
      @>
    : Branch End
    @>
  : Branch End
  @>
: Branch End
@>Conditional Branch: Variable [0019:X] == 30
  @>Conditional Branch: Variable [0020:Y] == 1
    @>Transfer Player:[001:Eagle's Crossing] (012,004), Down
    @>
  : Branch End
  @>
: Branch End
@>
```

This will allow the player to transition down to the new map and progress within the game. So, now you have a constant section to look forward to for each of the next few chapters (besides the town greeter blurb). Now, let's resume our work with the second level of our game's dungeon.

Static Encounters with Variable Enemy Troops

For the first level of our game, every monster event represented a troop of a single enemy. Erring on the side of easy at the start of a game is never a bad idea. However, the game will get dull rather quickly if the player is fighting a single enemy (especially later on, when he/she accompanied by a companion). One way to add a little diversity to enemy encounters is to make the event graphic represent a random number of enemies. How do we do this? It's very simple. I'll cover this in a few pages. For now, we have to define our enemy types for the Lower Catacombs. See Table 5-1.

Table 5-1. *A List of Possible Enemy Encounters in the Lower Catacombs*

Name	MHP	MMP	ATK	DEF	MAT	MDF	AGI	LUK	HIT%	EVA%	Attack Element
Bat	12	0	9	4	1	1	5	5	80	10	Pierce
Scorpion	14	0	10	5	1	1	2	2	75	0	Crush
Living Statue	50	0	15	5	1	1	1	8	80	0	Slash

■ **Note** Given that there's no actual Living Statue in RPG Maker VX Ace's (RMVXA's) stock graphics, I use the Paladin_m battle sprite.

While the enemies are stronger, they award more EXP and gold when defeated. The Living Statue enemies are activated when the player opens any of the chests inside the central tomb. Table 5-2 includes the item drop list and skills list for each of our new enemies.

Table 5-2. *The Item Drop and Skill List for the Enemies of the Lower Catacombs*

Name	EXP	G	Item Drop Slot 1 (Drop Chance)	Item Drop Slot 2 (Drop Chance)	Item Drop Slot 3 (Drop Chance)	Skill List (Rating)
Bat	6	8	Lesser Healing Potion (1/10)	None	None	Attack (5)
Scorpion	7	10	Antidote (1/5)	Lesser Healing Potion (1/10)	None	Attack (5), Poison Sting (4)
Living Statue	25	40	Gold Coin (1/2)	Return Crystal (1/4)	None	Attack (5)

The Scorpion is the first enemy in our game to have another usable skill besides the regular attack. Poison Sting has a Pierce-type element and a damage formula identical to that of the Attack skill (a.atk > b.def ? a.atk - b.def : 1). True to its name, the Poison Sting has a 30% chance of inflicting Poison if it connects with its target. Given that this is the first time we add a skill to an enemy, let me walk you through the process.

- Create Poison Sting. Remember that you can create new skills within the Skills tab. In my Database, Poison Sting is in the 21st skill slot.

- Go to the Enemies tab and create the Scorpion by assigning its parameters, rewards, and drops.

- Next, look at the Action Patterns section. Right-click and select Edit (or double left-click) the slot immediately below Attack.

- From the new dialog menu that appears, find the Poison Sting skill, then assign it a rating of 4.

Ratings determine the frequency with which an enemy uses a particular skill. For the sake of simplicity, just know that the Scorpion will favor using Attack over Poison Sting.

You can also see that I've given each enemy at least one possible item drop. This is a tendency that I will demonstrate throughout the rest of this book. After all, who doesn't enjoy the chance to get more loot? The Gold Coin is one of three similar items with the sole purpose of being sold to get some extra gold. I placed them in the three blank slots between the last spell scroll and the Catacomb Key. See Table 5-3 for the new item breakdown.

Table 5-3. *Our Game's Three Salable Items*

Item Name	Description	Price
Gold Coin	Can be exchanged for 10 gold pieces	20 G
Gold Nugget	Can be exchanged for 100 gold pieces	200 G
Gold Bars	Can be exchanged for 1000 gold pieces	2000 G

■ **Note** By default in RMVXA, items sell for half their value. So, to cite an example: If you want an item to sell for 500 gold, it must cost 1000 gold.

Now that we have established our level's enemies, we can actually place them on the map.

■ **Note** Don't forget to create the appropriate troops! You'll want two troops each for the Bats and Scorpions. One troop will have a single enemy, while the second will have two of the same enemy. The Living Statue only needs a single troop of one enemy.

The upper half of the level (which shares the same tileset as the Upper Catacombs) will have Bats. Additionally, we will place a total of four Living Statues in that area (two on each side of the area). The Scorpions will be located on the lower half of the level (which will share the same tileset as the Caves in the next chapter). So, how do we make an enemy encounter that has a variable amount of enemies? Let's look at the event we previously created for our Level 1 enemies.

Autonomous Movement
Type: Random
Speed: 3: x2 Slower
Freq: 3: Normal
Priority: Same as Characters
Trigger: Event Touch

Contents
```
@>Battle Processing: <troop> (where <troop> is the selected Troop; in this
case, Slime or Rat)
: If Win
  @>Erase Event
  @>
: If Escape
  @>Set Move Route: This event
  :                 : $>Wait: 300 frame(s)
  @>
: Branch End
@>
```

If we use a variable to store a random number and then use that number to check against a pair of conditional branches, we can determine how many enemies the troop will have. Here's the event I created for the Bat enemy.

Contents
```
Control Variables: [0004:d3] = Random No. (1...3)
@>Conditional Branch: Variable [0004:d3] < 3
  @>Battle Processing: Bat
  : If Win
    @>Erase Event
    @>
  : If Escape
    @>Set Move Route: This event
    :                 : $>Wait: 300 frame(s)
    @>
  : Branch End
  @>
: Branch End
@>Conditional Branch: Variable [0004:d3] == 3
  @>Battle Processing: Bat*2
  : If Win
    @>Erase Event
    @>
  : If Escape
    @>Set Move Route: This event
    :                 : $>Wait: 300 frame(s)
    @>
```

```
  : Branch End
  @>
: Branch End
@>
```

I use a variable named d3 (the shorthand nomenclature for three-sided dice), to hold a random number between 1 and 3. Then, I have the game check to see if d3 is less than 3 (which means it is equal to 1 or 2). In that case, the player is attacked by one Bat. If d3 is equal to 3, the player is attacked by a pair of Bats. Make the same type of event for the Scorpion enemy and then place it on the map. I placed a total of nine Bats and four Scorpions in the level. The Living Statue will have a simple encounter event, much like the Slimes and Rats of the first level. But, I'll talk more about our overpowered enemy later in the chapter.

Let's Create a Puzzle!

While the previous blocking door in our game was thwarted by a simple key, this particular door will require some more effort. Upon the player interacting with it, the door will ask for its value and leave the player to give a number without any hint save one: if the player writes in an incorrect answer, the gate will shout: "Incorrect! Seek the knowledge of the stone tablets!" We'll create this puzzle in the same order that the player should solve it.

The Stone Tablets

After getting told to seek the stone tablets, the average would-be puzzle solver would try to find said tablets. There will be seven of them along the walls at the northern end of the level. They all share the graphic displayed in Figure 5-2 and have the same first line of "The value of the statues."

Figure 5-2. The Stone Tablet graphic from tab B of the Dungeon tileset

Here's a list of the seven hints that should be spread among the tablets.

- From north to south

- Each set gives a part/To their number

- Is a number in digits three

- Each side is one number

- Is not a sum

- The broken bust/Valued zero

- Subtract right from left

The slash in two of the bullet points signifies a line break. Let's use the longest hint as an example of how the text events should be set up.

```
Priority: Same as Characters
Trigger: Action Button
@>Text: -, -, Normal, Bottom
:      : The value of the statues
:      : Each set gives a part
:      : to their number
```

The Statues and the Gate

We give quite a few hints concerning statues, and that is where the player should head next. When all of the hints are examined as a whole, the player should realize that each set of statues represents a single three-digit number. Players are to subtract the value of the right-hand side from that of the left-hand side to get the gate's value and solve the riddle. The gate event is two pages long. The first page handles the puzzle logic, while the second page is the open door event that is triggered after the player successfully solves the puzzle.

```
Page 1 of 2
Graphic: Upper-left corner graphic of !$Gate2
Options: Uncheck Walking Anim. Toggle Direction Fix.
Priority: Same as Characters
Trigger: Action Button
@>Text: -, -, Normal, Bottom
:      : A booming voice resonates from the gate.
@>Text: -, -, Normal, Bottom
:      : Answer my riddle and you may pass!
@>Text: -, -, Normal, Bottom
:      : What is my value?
@>Input Number: [0005:GateRiddle], 3 digits
@>Conditional Branch: Variable [0005:GateRiddle] == 192
  @>Text: -, -, Normal, Bottom
  :      : Correct! You may pass!
```

```
@>Set Move Route: This event (Wait)
:                : $>Turn Left
:                : $>Wait: 3 frame(s)
:                : $>Turn Right
:                : $>Wait: 3 frame(s)
:                : $>Turn Up
:                : $>Through ON
@>Control Self Switch: A =ON
@>Play SE: 'Open2', 80, 100
@>
: Branch End
@>Conditional Branch: Variable [0005:GateRiddle] != 192
  @>Text: -, -, Normal, Bottom
  :     : Incorrect! Seek the knowledge of the stone tablets!
  @>Control Variables: [0005:GateRiddle] = 0
  @>
: Branch End
@>
```

■ **Note**   An easier way to add the preceding event to your game is by using the Door Quick Event and edit it accordingly. It will even add both of the necessary event pages for you!

This event uses the Input Number event command, which had not been used up to now. As its name states, Input Number allows the player to type in a number of up to X digits in size, where X in this case is 3. Then, we check to see if the player has given the correct solution (192). If he/she has, the gate opens, allowing him/her to pass into the central tomb. Otherwise, the variable will be set to 0 once again, and the player will be told to seek the stone tablets.

Page 2 of 2
Graphic: Lower-left corner graphic of !$Gate2
Condition: Self Switch A is ON
Priority: Same as Characters
Trigger: Action Button
Options: Uncheck Walking Anim. Check Direction Fix and Through.
No Contents

■ **Caution**   Toggling the Through check box is important in this particular instance. Otherwise, the player cannot pass through the opened gate. While comparatively tame, you want to have Direction Fix on as well, or graphical glitches can occur.

How does the player know to solve for 192? Well, taking the hints provided by the stone tablets, the right set of statues represents a single three-digit number, while the left set of statues represents a second three-digit number. The broken bust counts as zero. Thus, the right side is 405, while the left side is 213. The solution is as easy as subtracting 213 from 405. Last, you may be wondering how this all looks in-game. After all, there's a one-space gap that I didn't cover with an event. (You may have noticed it in Figure 5-1. I'll be providing a zoomed-in screenshot of it in Figure 5-3.) Take a look at Figure 5-3.

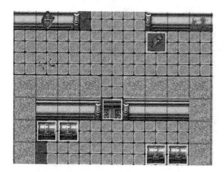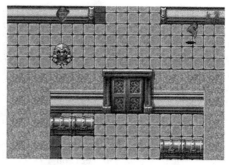

Figure 5-3. *A screenshot (right) of the area surrounding the gate in RMVXA's editor and one (left) of the area surrounding the gate during an actual play-through*

The player wouldn't know that there's a wall gap one space above the gate's event, but for the fact that the gap is the only reason he/she can interact with the gate at all. Looks pretty neat, if I do say so myself.

■ **Note** As with the Catacomb Key in Level 1, you could award the player some experience for solving the gate puzzle. I'd personally give him/her 50 EXP.

The Treasure of the Lower Catacombs

Once players have made their way past the gate, they will find themselves in the central tomb. A small opening at the far side of the tomb eventually leads to the entrance to the Caves, the third dungeon level of our game. Notably, there are a total of 16 chests ripe for the taking. Or are they? There are three types of chests in this room.

1. **Empty chests.** Nine of the chests in this room are empty.

2. **Character-specific chests.** Three of the chests in this room have contents dependent on the player's character.

3. **Standard chests.** Four chests in this room have the same contents regardless of the player's character.

When the player tries to open *any* of the chests, they will receive a message about a "mysterious aura surrounding the chest." If the player opens the chest, the four Living Statues come to life and make their way to the player's position as fast as they can. Once the player has opened a chest, there are no further penalties for opening the other 15. In fact, the player will want to bite the bullet and open all of the chests, as they will contain items that may keep him/her alive against his/her overly strong foes. I will provide code for how a standard chest should look. We have already discussed how to create character-specific chests, and empty chests are functionally identical to standard chests.

Page 1 of 2
Graphic: Closed steel treasure chest in the upper-right corner of the !Chest graphic set.
Options: Direction Fix
Priority: Same as Characters
Trigger: Action Button
Contents:

```
@>Conditonal Branch: Switch [0008:StatuesAwake] == ON
  @>Play SE: 'Chest', 80, 100
  @>Set Move Route: This event (Wait)
  :                : $>Direction Fix OFF
  :                : $>Turn Left
  :                : $>Wait: 3 frame(s)
  :                : $>Turn Right
  :                : $>Wait: 3 frame(s)
  @>Control Self Switch: A =ON
  @>Change Gold: + 200
  @>Text: -, -, Normal, Bottom
  :      : 200\G were found!
  @>
: Branch End
@>Conditonal Branch: Switch [0008:StatuesAwake] == OFF
  @>Text: -, -, Normal, Bottom
  :      : A mysterious aura surrounds this chest. Do you wish
  :      : to open it?
  @>Show Choices: Yes, No
  : When [Yes]
    @>Play SE: 'Chest', 80, 100
    @>Set Move Route: This event (Wait)
    :                : $>Direction Fix OFF
    :                : $>Turn Left
    :                : $>Wait: 3 frame(s)
    :                : $>Turn Right
    :                : $>Wait: 3 frame(s)
    @>Control Self Switch: A =ON
    @>Change Gold: + 200
    @>Text: -, -, Normal, Bottom
    :      : 200\G were found!
    @>Control Switches: [0008:StatuesAwake] = ON
```

```
@>Text: -, -, Normal, Bottom
 :       : The aura dissipates as the ancient statues of the
 :       : Catacombs come to life!
 @>
: When [No]
 @>
: Branch End
@>
: Branch End
@>
```

Here we have a new switch called StatuesAwake. While the player has not opened any of the chests, it remains off. Once the player opens a chest, it toggles on, and the Living Statues are activated. I'll cover our strong enemies in the next section. For now, here's a list of the treasure to be placed within the seven treasure chests that are meant to contain items. *Character-specific chest contents are listed in the form X/Y/Z, where X is Palnor's item, Y is Gust's item, and Z is Feylia's item.*

- Bronze Full Plate/Hauberk/250 Gold

- Iron Sword/Iron Bow/Obsidian Staff

- 200 Gold/Iron Arrow/Scroll of Chill

- 1 Return Crystal

- 1 Healing Potion

- 2 Antidotes

- 1 Panacea

The Living Statues

It is not uncommon for dungeon crawlers to have trapped chests. While our living statue trap is far more subtle than an arrow or a fireball to the face, it still fits under that umbrella. The player has to decide whether they fight back or escape the level (preferably into the Caves, as retreating into the Upper Catacombs would just perpetuate the problem). Given the strength and origin of the statues, it is best if they are permanently defeated after the player beats them in battle. You could make them re-spawn, but that would be rather cruel. So, where exactly are these living statues located? There are two on each side of the level, in the positions displayed in Figure 5-4.

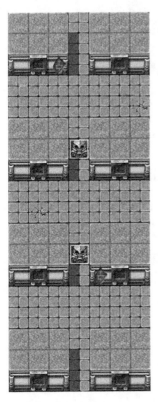

Figure 5-4. *The location of the Living Statue enemies on the left side of the level. Since the upper half of the level has a mirrored appearance, there are two more in the same relative location of the right side as well.*

All that is left is to create the Living Statue events themselves. The event will have three pages. See Figure 5-5 for a screenshot of the graphic used for the Living Statue enemy before I write out the event. You can find this particular graphic in the People4 graphic set.

Figure 5-5. *The graphic used to represent the Living Statue enemies*

Page 1 of 3
Graphic: *See Figure 5-5*
Priority: Same as Characters
Trigger: Action Button
@>Text: -, -, Normal, Bottom
:   : You see a stone statue. It looks strangely lifelike.
Page 2 of 3
Graphic: *Same as previous page*
Condition: 0008:StatuesAwake is ON
Autonomous Movement
Type: Approach
Speed: 5: x2 Faster
Freq: 4: Higher
Priority: Same as Characters
Trigger: Event Touch
@>Battle Processing: Living Statue
: If Win
  @>Control Self Switch: A =ON
  @>
: If Escape
  @>Set Move Route: This event
  :   : $>Wait: 300 frame(s)
  @>
: Branch End
@>

Page 3 of 3
Condition: Self Switch A is ON
No Graphic
Priority: Below Characters
Trigger: Action Button
No Contents

There's not much difference between the Living Statue and our Level 1 enemies once the statues activate. The first page covers what happens if the player interacts with one of the statues before trying to open one of the central tomb's chests. The player receives a slightly foreboding message, but little else. However, once the Living Statues awaken, they will try to converge on the player's position.

■ **Note**   And I do mean *try*. Unless you have very linear locations, enemies with the Approach movement type may get trapped in some place or another trying to reach the player's position.Unlike every other enemy type that we have created so far, the Living Statue has a movement type of Approach. They will also move at a quicker rate than our other enemies, making looting the other chests as fast as possible highly imperative for the player. With all of that set up, we are done with this level (and, by extension, with this chapter).

Summary

During the course of this chapter, we worked on the lower half of the catacombs of Eagle's Crossing. We added monster encounters that have varying amount of enemies, a puzzle gate blocking the way to the next level and lots of treasure, and strong enemies that activate in response to the player's actions (opening treasure chests). In the next chapter, I will cover the Caves of our dungeon crawler.

CHAPTER 6

■ ■ ■

The Caves

In this chapter, we will be working on our dungeon's third level, the Caves. Our game's first boss monster will be encountered here, and the player will have to deal with flipping switches to reach a chest containing an item required to progress. In addition, a new type of key will be required to open certain doors within the level.

The Caves

The Caves are a network of interconnected tunnels that exist below Eagle's Crossing. It has been many years since anyone has found his way down there. Who knows what horrors lie in wait?

If the player has cleared out both previous levels in their entirety, the experience gained should put his/her character at Level 5. If the player defeats only one Living Statue (or none), he/she will be at Level 4. In either case, this is what I will cover during this chapter.

- **Random roaming encounters**: The player can see an enemy sprite on the map. However, what enemy will spawn if the player engages? It could be one of three different enemy types!

- **Random chests**: We have chests with variable contents already, and we're going to discuss random enemies, so why not discuss random chests as well?

- **Doors and more doors**: This level will have doors that require a key to open, as well as doors that open when the player pulls the correct switch.

- **Vehicles**: Or, rather, vehicle, in the singular. To get to the Western Pixies' Forest (Level 4), the player will require a way to cross the small lake that separates the rest of the level from the way down.

What Does the Town Greeter Have to Say?

The flavor text below is what you should add to the town greeter for this particular dungeon level.

> *The townsfolk are in awe. Caves under their town—who would have thought? Now, if you got there through the catacombs, you do have to wonder, who, or what, tunneled through the area?*

Foreshadowing is the spice of life, don't you agree? The *what*, incidentally, is our game's first boss. But more on that later.

Level Overview

As is usual, let's start by creating the map. Make a 64×47 sized map with the Dungeon tileset, the Dungeon8 BGM, and a DirtCave and DirtCave battleback. Then, see Figure 6-1 for a screenshot of the level in completed form.

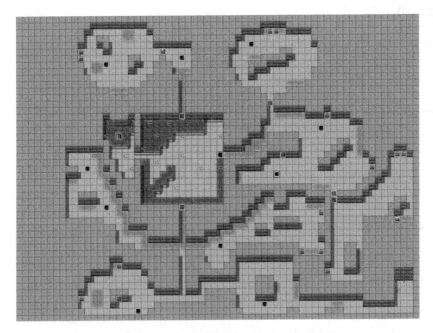

Figure 6-1. *The Caves of our game's dungeon*

> ■ **Note**   The tiles used to create the map are Wall (Dirt Cave), Ground (Dirt Cave), Water, and Dark Ground (Grass Maze).

The player arrives at the Caves via the rope hanging in the lower-right corner of the area. There are a total of 11 enemy encounters and 16 chests on the map. Much like in the previous chapter, let's start this one off by creating the transfer events for the previous level.

Creating Transfer Events for the Lower Catacombs

Like the Upper Catacombs above them, the Lower Catacombs have a pair of staircases (or, rather, a single staircase and a hole). Before creating the transfer events, you should take a moment and make sure that the hole is passable. By default, the hole tile that I used (located in tab A of the Dungeon tileset) does *not* have passability. How can we change the passability of an object? Roughly in the same way we can edit its Terrain Tags (which I will cover in the next chapter, in fact).

- Open the Database and go to the Tilesets tab.

- From there, left-click the Dungeon tileset.

- Next, find the hole used in the dungeon level. The hole of interest is the fifth tile of the third row of tab A.

- If, for some reason, it isn't set to that option already, click the Passage button on the right-hand part of the menu.

- You will notice that the hole has an X. An X symbolizes impassibility. Click that tile once and note how it changes to an O. Tiles that have an O are passable.

Now that our player can actually walk on top of the hole, here's the relevant Parallel Process transfer event you'll need for the Lower Catacombs.

```
Trigger: Parallel Process
@>Control Variables: [0019:X] = Player's Map X
@>Control Variables: [0020:Y] = Player's Map Y
@>Conditional Branch: Variable [0019:X] == 55
  @>Conditional Branch: Variable [0020:Y] == 42
    @>Conditional Branch: Self Switch B == OFF
      @>Control Variables: [0001:DeepestDungeonFloor] = 3
      @>Control Self Switch: B =ON
      @>Transfer Player:[009:Level 3] (061,042), Down
    : Else
      @>Transfer Player:[009:Level 3] (061,042), Down
      @>
```

```
      : Branch End
      @>
    : Branch End
   @>
  : Branch End
@>Conditional Branch: Variable [0019:X] == 29
  @>Conditional Branch: Variable [0020:Y] == 3
    @>Transfer Player:[007:Level 1] (030,002), Down
    @>
   : Branch End
  @>
: Branch End
@>
```

Now we can start this chapter in earnest. The first topic of discussion will be the enemies the player can fight in the Caves.

The Enemies of the Caves

In Level 1, we had fixed enemy encounters. In Level 2, we had fixed enemy encounters of variable sizes, dependent on the value of a random variable. Now, as the player enters Level 3, he/she will find him-/herself staring at shapeless monsters that could be one of three distinct enemy types. See Table 6-1 for a table of the monsters that the player will fight in the Caves. (Kerberos is the boss monster and should prove a hefty challenge to any of the main characters.)

Table 6-1. *A List of the Enemies the Player Will Face in the Caves*

Name	MHP	MMP	ATK	DEF	MAT	MDF	AGI	LUK	HIT%	EVA%	Attack Element
Spider	20	0	12	6	1	1	4	4	85	5	Crush
Imp	18	12	7	4	5	5	8	8	70	10	Slash
Snake	22	0	14	7	1	1	5	5	85	5	Slash
Kerberos	100	60	18	10	10	5	10	10	90	5	Crush

Table 6-2 provides the experience and gold rewards and item drop and skill lists for our four enemies.

Table 6-2. *Item Drops and Skills for the Cave's Enemies*

Name	EXP	G	Item Drop Slot 1 (Drop Chance)	Item Drop Slot 2 (Drop Chance)	Item Drop Slot 3 (Drop Chance)	Skill List (Rating)
Spider	15	20	Lesser Healing Potion (1/10)	Return Crystal (1/20)	None	Attack (5), Poison Bite (4)
Imp	17	22	Lesser Magic Potion (1/8)	Scroll of Blaze (1/20)	None	Attack (5), Blaze (4)
Snake	19	25	Antidote (1/4)	Scroll of Poison Cloud (1/25)	None	Attack (5), Poison Bite (5)
Kerberos	250	250	Heart Amulet (1/1)	None	None	Rend (5), Bicker (10), Blaze (7), Smog Breath (7)

The experience and gold rewards may seem rather high, but it is a common dungeon crawler convention to scale in this way. After all, you want to keep your players pushing ever deeper into the dungeon, not grinding weaker enemies to get some extra levels and equipment. As a boss, Kerberos has a total of four skills he can use. Also, he will be vulnerable to Ice and immune to Fire. I will cover the effects of his item drop later in the chapter. See Table 6-3 for a breakdown of the new skills created for this chapter.

Table 6-3. *List of New Skills Created for This Dungeon Level*

Skill Name	Element	Description	Damage Formula	Notes
Poison Bite	Pierce	Deals damage and may poison an enemy	a.atk > b.def ? a.atk - b.def : 1	Used by Spiders and Snakes. 40% chance to poison the target
Rend	None	A fierce attack that lowers the target's DEF by 25% for four turns	a.atk > b.def ? a.atk - b.def : 1	Used by Kerberos. Has the *Add Debuff [DEF] 4 Turns* Effect.

(*continued*)

Table 6-3. (*continued*)

Skill Name	Element	Description	Damage Formula	Notes
Bicker	None	A pointless argument that causes the user to skip a turn	N/A	Used by Kerberos, granting the player a respite every few turns. Has a Scope of None and a use message of ['s heads bicker amongst themselves!]. In-game, the message would look like so: "Kerberos's heads bicker amongst themselves!"
Smog Breath	Fire	A possibly blinding exhalation that targets all enemies	`2 + a.mat > b.mdf ?` `2 + a.mat - b.mdf` `: 1`	Used by Kerberos. 50% chance to blind targets. Has a Scope of All Enemies.

■ **Note** You can use the Element Rate Feature (which is one of the Features in the list that comes up when you right-click the Features section of Database tabs that have one and select Edit) to set weaknesses and immunities for enemies (and equipment). Kerberos should have Element Rates of [Fire] * 0% and [Ice] * 200%, meaning that he takes no damage from fire-based attacks and double damage from ice.

Last, but definitely not least, check Figure 6-2 to see a screenshot of Kerberos's action patterns, so that you can note the timing for each of his skills.

Action Patterns

Skill	Condition	R
Rend	Always	4
Bicker	Turn No. 4+4*X	10
Blaze	Turn No. 2+2*X	7
Smog Breath	Turn No. 2+2*X	7

Figure 6-2. *The Action Patterns window for Kerberos*

Rend is Kerberos's normal attack, and the only skill with a condition of Always. If the activation conditions for his other abilities are not valid during a certain turn, you can expect to see him use Rend. On every even turn that's not a multiple of four (2, 6, 10, etc.), Kerberos will use either Blaze or Smog Breath (at a 50% chance of using either ability). On every fourth turn, Kerberos's heads will have a little argument, causing the boss to skip that turn. I will cover Kerberos's special encounter later in the chapter.

Random Roaming Enemies

For now, let's cover the regular enemy encounters that will be placed around the area. Because we want to have three possible enemy encounters within a single event, we should use a sprite with an undefined shape, similar to how some role-playing games (RPGs) have handled roaming encounters (world map encounters in *Tales of Symphonia* come to mind). See Figure 6-3 for the sprite I'll use for these encounters.

Graphic

Figure 6-3. *The indistinct enemy encounter sprite*

■ **Note** You can find the sprite I'm using within the Monster1 graphic set.

As for the event itself, what if I told you that you can tweak the encounter event used for the Bats and Scorpions of Level 2 to make this one? Perhaps you already suspected as much. After all, the only difference between the two events is their intent. The Level 2 events were coded to make a troop of either one or two appear. We want the Level 3 events to randomly select one of three size-one troops. The following is how the event should look (and I fully encourage you to draw parallels between this event and the one in the previous chapter):

```
@>Control Variables: [0004:d3] = Random No. (1...6)
@>Conditional Branch: Variable [0004:d3] <= 2
  @>Battle Processing: Spider
  : If Win
    @>Erase Event
    @>
  : If Escape
    @>Set Move Route: This event
    :                 : $>Wait: 300 frame(s)
    @>
  : Branch End
  @>
: Branch End
@>Conditional Branch: Variable [0004:d3] >= 3
  @>Conditional Branch: Variable [0004:d3] <= 5
    @>Battle Processing: Imp
    : If Win
      @>Erase Event
      @>
    : If Escape
      @>Set Move Route: This event
      :                 : $>Wait: 300 frame(s)
      @>
    : Branch End
  @>
  : Branch End
  @>
: Branch End
@>Conditional Branch: Variable [0004:d3] == 6
  @>Battle Processing: Snake
  : If Win
    @>Erase Event
    @>
  : If Escape
    @>Set Move Route: This event
    :                 : $>Wait: 300 frame(s)
    @>
  : Branch End
  @>
: Branch End
@>
```

104

■ **Note** I even use the same variable (d3) as before! As long as you don't need the variable's information for some other important purpose, it doesn't really matter what the variable is named.

Take a little time now to create the enemies and their associated troops (we're looking at one troop for each enemy, including the boss, and each troop should have a single enemy). As I did not change the name of any of the enemies, you can find their battle sprites just by looking for the appropriately named battler graphics. When the player bumps into one of these enemy encounters, the game picks a random number between one and six and saves the result to the d3 variable. If the result is one or two, the player is attacked by a Spider. If the result is three to five, the player must do battle with an Imp. If the result happens to be six, the player fights a Snake. Now, you may be wondering what will happen if you escape from battle and then re-engage the same encounter. In the event's current state, it'll pick another random number, and you may find yourself fighting a different enemy. If that bothers you, there's a way to make the initial roll permanent for a specific event. What you'll want to do is the following:

- When the player and event meet for the first time, use the random variable to get a number, as usual.

- Flip a self-switch dependent on the number result.

- The enemy encounter is determined by the self-switch that has been flipped.

In essence, it should look something like the following:

Page 1 of 2
```
@>Conditional Branch: Self Switch A = OFF
  @>Control Variables: [0004:d3] = Random No. (1...6)
  @>Conditional Branch: Variable [0004:d3] <= 2
    @>Control Self Switch: A =ON
    @>Control Self Switch: B =ON
  : Branch End
  @>Conditional Branch: Variable [0004:d3] >= 3
    @>Conditional Branch: Variable [0004:d3] <= 5
      @>Control Self Switch: A =ON
      @>Control Self Switch: C =ON
      : Branch End
    @>
  : Branch End
  @>Conditional Branch: Variable [0004:d3] == 6
    @>Control Self Switch: A =ON
    @>Control Self Switch: D =ON
  : Branch End
```

Page 2 of 2
Condition: Self Switch A is ON
```
@>Conditional Branch: Self Switch B == ON
  @>Battle Processing: Spider
  : If Win
    @>Erase Event
    @>
  : If Escape
    @>Set Move Route: This event
    :                 : $>Wait: 300 frame(s)
    @>
  : Branch End
  @>
: Branch End
@>Conditional Branch: Self Switch C == ON
  @>Battle Processing: Imp
  : If Win
    @>Erase Event
    @>
  : If Escape
    @>Set Move Route: This event
    :                 : $>Wait: 300 frame(s)
    @>
  : Branch End
@>
: Branch End
@>Conditional Branch: Self Switch D == ON
  @>Battle Processing: Snake
  : If Win
    @>Erase Event
    @>
  : If Escape
    @>Set Move Route: This event
    :                 : $>Wait: 300 frame(s)
    @>
  : Branch End
  @>
: Branch End
@>
```

That will give those events a sense of permanence, should you desire it. Copy-paste the event to its relative locations, as shown in Figure 6-1, and let's move on.

Doors!

In the Caves, there are five doors divided into two different types. Two of the doors require keys, while the other three open via the use of switches scattered around the level. We have already tackled doors of the former type in Chapter 3 (the Upper Catacombs), but the event I will be using this time is slightly different.

Doors That Require Keys

First, here's page 2 of the door event we used back in Chapter 3. We'll be using it as a point of reference for our new door events.

```
Condition: Item 036:Catacomb Key exists
Contents
@>Play SE: 'Open1', 80, 100
@>Set Move Route: This event (Wait)
:                 : $>Turn Left
:                 : $>Wait: 3 frame(s)
:                 : $>Turn Right
:                 : $>Wait: 3 frame(s)
:                 : $>Turn Up
:                 : $>Through ON
@>Set Move Route: Player (Skip, Wait)
:                 : $>1 Step Forward
@>Erase Event
@>
```

Our new door events will be two pages long and work somewhat differently than the preceding.

- The keys used for these doors are single-use. That is, they break after they open the door.

- The door will remain open permanently, in contrast with the catacombs door that locks itself when the player leaves the level.

- We will handle the door's logic in the same page on which we place the door description (our other door event divided those between two pages).

See Figure 6-4 for a screenshot of the location of the two doors (as well as one of the enemy encounters).

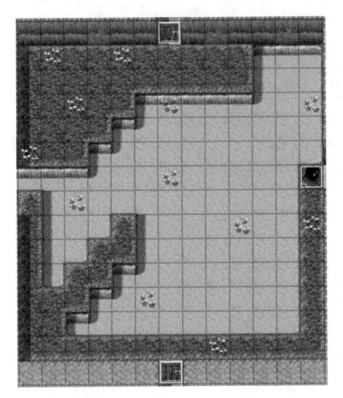

Figure 6-4. *The lake near the central part of the Caves. Note the iron doors blocking the northern and southern corridors*

The graphic used for our two doors can be found in !Door2 (specifically, the tile two squares below the upper-left corner of the graphic set). Here are the two event pages for our iron doors:

Page 1 of 2
Options: Toggle Direction Fix
Priority: Same as Characters
Trigger: Action Button
```
@>Text: -, -, Normal, Bottom
:     : You see an iron door with a lock.
@>Conditional Branch: [Iron Key] in Inventory
  @>Text: -, -, Normal, Bottom
  :     : Do you wish to open the door?
  @>Show Choices: Yes, No
  : When [Yes]
    @>Text: -, -, Normal, Bottom
    :     : You twist the key in the keyhole and it opens, but
    :     : not before snapping the key!
```

```
   @>Change Items: [Iron Key], -1
   @>Control Self Switch: A =ON
   @>
 : When [No]
   @>
 : Branch End
 @>
: Else
 @>
: Branch End
@>
```

Page 2 of 2
Condition: Self Switch A is ON
No Graphic
No Contents

■ **Note**   If you don't use Direction Fix for this event, you will see the graphic for the door change before your very eyes.

When the player interacts with the iron door, we have the game tell him/her what he/she is looking at. Then, if the player has an Iron Key in his/her inventory, it will provide the option of opening the door. If the player does not have the key, the door will open for the cost of a key. Once the door is open, we flip self-switch A, which causes page 2 to trigger, removing the iron door graphic for the duration of the game. This level will have a pair of Iron Keys that will be used for precisely this purpose.

■ **Note**   I'll cover the Iron Keys later on, when I discuss the treasure chests and their contents. Table 6-4 will contain a list of items to add to the game's Database, Iron Keys included.

Doors That Open with Switches

At the event level, making a door that opens with a switch is essentially the same as making a door that requires a key. The only real difference lies in how we structure our sequence of events. Rather than have a single door that requires an item, we have a door that requires a switch to be set, and we have the lever that has to be pulled (and sets the appropriate switch when pulled). Figure 6-5 shows the map of the Caves with the doors and switches marked accordingly.

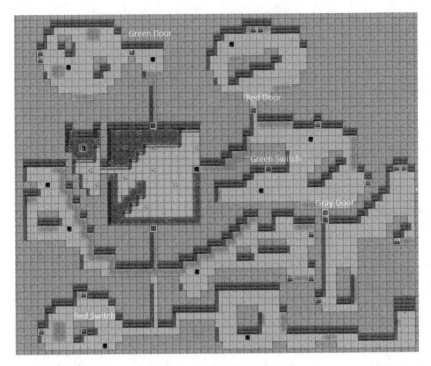

Figure 6-5. *The Cave map, with added annotations*

When the player pulls the red switch, the red door opens. Likewise, when the green switch is pulled, the green door opens. When both switches have been pulled, the gray door will open as well. I will cover the process of eventing the red door and red switch and leave the green-colored events as an exercise for you. (The finished article can be found in the download pack, if you want to check what you've done.) Both the switch and the door are two-page affairs, as they have before and after states. Here's the red switch event located at 016,043:

Page 1 of 2
Graphic: Red lever in the upper-right corner of !Switch2
Priority: Same as Characters
Trigger: Action Button
```
@>Text: -, -, Normal, Bottom
:       : You see a red lever. Will you pull it?
@>Show Choices: Yes, No
: When [Yes]
  @>Set Move Route: This event (Wait)
  :                : $>Turn Left
  :                : $>Wait: 5 frame(s)
  :                : $>Turn Right
  :                : $>Wait: 5 frame(s)
```

```
:                   : $>Turn Up
:                   : $>Wait: 5 frame(s)
@>Control Switches: [0011:RedSwitch] = ON
@>Text: -, -, Normal, Bottom
:        : You hear a door open in the distance!
  @>
: When [No]
  @>
: Branch End
@>
```

Page 2 of 2
Graphic: Red lever three squares below the upper-right corner of !Switch2
Condition: 0011:RedSwitch is ON
Options: Toggle Direction Fix
Priority: Same as Characters
Trigger: Action Button
```
@>Text: -, -, Normal, Bottom
:        : You have already pulled this lever.
```

■ **Note**   I toggle Direction Fix in page 2, to prevent the lever graphic from temporarily glitching out when the player interacts with it. It is not necessary to do this for page 1. In fact, if you set Direction Fix to **on** in the first page of the switch event, it won't animate at all (just suddenly be set to the end position when the page is switched).

You can create the green switch event in the same way (the graphics used for the green switch are six squares to the right of the red lever graphics). All you would have to do is replace the graphics and the switch that is flipped on (GreenSwitch instead of RedSwitch). The green switch event is located at 042,021. Now, let's tackle the red door event.

Page 1 of 2
Graphic: Sixth graphic in the top row of !Door2
Options: Toggle Direction Fix
Priority: Same as Characters
Trigger: Action Button
```
@>Text: -, -, Normal, Bottom
:        : You see a red door made out of stone.
```

Page 2 of 2
Condition: 0011:RedSwitch is ON
No Graphic
No Contents

There's really not much to it. If the player finds the door in a raised position (in other words, before pulling the red lever), he/she will receive a short message when he/she interacts with it. Otherwise, the door will not be there at all, and the player can pass through. The red door is located at 040,013. The graphic used for the green door is three tiles below and one tile right from the red door graphic. It should be really easy to find, given that it is the only one of the four green door tiles that is set sideways. The green door is located at 023,005.

I decided to use a three-page event for the gray door, in the interest of being efficient. You want the player to know whether a door has been unlocked by their actions, and the best way to do so is to have a different message display when the player pulls the second switch. I'm going to use an Autorun event for this purpose, but instead of dedicating an event slot to it, I'll just make it so that the second page of the gray door event has an Autorun trigger. The gray door is located at 050,027. Without further ado, here's the gray door event code:

Page 1 of 3
Graphic: Fourth graphic in the top row of !Door2
Options: Toggle Direction Fix
Priority: Same as Characters
Trigger: Action Button
@>Text: -, -, Normal, Bottom
:   : You see a gray door made out of stone.

Page 2 of 3
Conditions: 0011:RedSwitch is ON, 0012: GreenSwitch is ON
Graphic: (You can leave it blank or use the same one as in Page 1)
Priority: (any of the three is fine)
Trigger: Autorun
@>Text: -, -, Normal, Bottom
:   : You hear another door open in the distance.
@>Control Self Switch: A =ON
@>

Page 3 of 3
Conditions: 0011:RedSwitch is ON, 0012: GreenSwitch is ON, Self Switch A is ON
Graphic: None
Priority: Below Characters
Trigger: Action Button
No Contents

The first page is identical to that of the red and green doors. Where it gets interesting is when both the red and green switches have been flipped. Page 2 triggers automatically at that point, telling the player that another door has opened in the distance and flipping the self-switch that makes the gray door event move on to page 3, which is the same blank page that the other two doors have. With that set up, it's time to talk about this level's loot!

The Cave's Treasure

The Caves are home to a whopping 15 chests, the most important of which are the two chests containing Iron Keys and the single metallic chest that contains an item that will be essential for the player's continued progression. Following is the list of treasure that should be divided within the 14 regular chests of the dungeon level. *The contents of the first three chests are determined by the player character (Palnor/Gust/Feylia). The contents of the next three chests are randomly determined. The last group of items are for nonspecific chests that will have the same rewards for all characters.*

- Power Amulet/Eagle Amulet/Defense Amulet

- Iron Chestplate/Iron Helm/400 Gold

- Iron Greatsword/500 Gold/Scroll of Immolate

- 100 Gold (60%)/500 Gold (30%)/Gold Bars (10%)

- 1 Healing Potion (40%)/2 Healing Potions (30%)/3 Healing Potions (20%)

- 1 Antidote (50%)/1 Panacea (30%)/1 Phoenix Tears (20%)

- 1 Phoenix Tears

- 1000 Gold

- 2 Eye Drops

- 1 Panacea

- 2 Antidotes

- 2 Iron Keys

You're free to put the treasure where you like in the level. The only hints, if you will, that I will offer concerning what should go where are the following:

- The metallic chest beyond the gray door will contain a special item called the Magic Oar. It uses a common event that will be discussed in a bit.

- The two Iron Keys should be located before the first iron door. There are a total of five chests that meet this condition. After all, what good is a key if it's locked behind the door it's meant to open?

- The greater rewards (such as the amulets) should be located in the harder-to-reach spots. I recommend placing most of them in the areas behind the red and green doors.

- The three bullets in the treasure list with percentage-based drops will be covered in the next section, so feel free to fill those after reading that far.

With all of that out of the way, it's time to add the new items to our game. See Table 6-4 for the list of items that should be added to our game's Database, along with where in the Database they go.

■ **Note** From here on, you should add new items to the end of their respective Database sections. So, the Amulets would be placed after the Mythril Arrow, while the two new Key Items would be placed after the Catacomb Key.

Table 6-4. *List of Items to Be Added to the Database*

Name	Description	Price	Item Type
Power Amulet	Increases the wearer's ATK by 5	1000 G	Armors (Accessory)
Eagle Amulet	Increases the wearer's ATK by 3 and HIT by 5%	1000 G	Armors (Accessory)
Defense Amulet	Increases the wearer's DEF and MDF by 5	1000 G	Armors (Accessory)
Heart Amulet	Increases the wearer's HP by 15	1000 G	Armors (Accessory)
Iron Key	Used to open iron doors	0 G	Items (Key Item)
Magic Oar	Calls a canoe in front of the user. Only works if the user is facing shallow water	0 G	Items (Key Item)

■ **Note** While little more than a semantic difference, you can differentiate regular items from important ones via the Item Type drop-down for any given item. Key Items are meant to be important items in your game.

Random Treasure

So, we have three chests in the previous section that have random probabilities for each item drop. We can handle this in the same way that we handled our enemy encounters. This time, we'll have d3 roll a random number from one to ten. I'll create the random treasure chest for the first of the three chests. You should be able to adapt the following event for the other two random chests.

```
@>Control Variables: [0004:d3] = Random No. (1...10)
@>Play SE: 'Chest', 80, 100
@>Set Move Route: This event (Wait)
:                 : $>Direction Fix OFF
:                 : $>Turn Left
:                 : $>Wait: 3 frame(s)
:                 : $>Turn Right
:                 : $>Wait: 3 frame(s)
@>Conditional Branch: Variable [0004:d3] <= 5
  @>Change Items: [Antidote], + 1
  @>Text: -, -, Normal, Bottom
  :     : Received Antidote!
  @>
: Branch End
@>Conditional Branch: Variable [0004:d3] > 6
  @>Conditional Branch: Variable [0004:d3] <= 8
    @>Change Items: [Panacea] + 1
    @>Text: -, -, Normal, Bottom
    :     : Received Panacea!
    @>
  : Branch End
  @>
: Branch End
@>
@>Conditional Branch: Variable [0004:d3] >= 9
  @>Change Items [Phoenix Tears], + 1
  @>Text: -, -, Normal, Bottom
  :     : Received Phoenix Tears!
  @>
: Branch End
@>Control Self Switch: A =ON
@>
```

I am able to streamline the preceding event owing to the fact that the chest opening animation and self-switch toggle occur no matter what item the player receives. So, instead of placing the Set Move Route and Control Self Switch event commands in triplicate, I can just have the chest open and then give the player the appropriate item, based on the random variable roll.

■ **Note**   Because I gave the percentage values in multiples of 10, we can use a variable that can roll from 1 to 10. Alternately, you could use a variable that goes up to 100 and then add a zero to each of the conditional branches. I tend to err toward the most intuitive solution whenever possible, but there are multiple ways to roll random numbers that will give the same result.

The Magic Oar

Past the gray door, the player will eventually find a special chest. It has the same graphic as the tomb chests in Level 2 and contains a very useful item. When used from the inventory, it will spawn a canoe in front of the character, but only if he/she is facing shallow water. Otherwise, the canoe will not appear, and an error message will be displayed. Before we populate the relevant chest, let's create the common event that will trigger when the item is used. This common event will require the following:

- Three variables. We already have two to store the player's x and y coordinates. We need a third to store the player's current map ID.

- The use of the Get Location Info and Set Vehicle Location event commands.

- Setting the Terrain Tag of the Water tile to 1.

All things considered, the common event is actually very easy to create. In fact, the only thing that could give pause is determining whether the tile in front of the player is shallow water, hence the reason for using Terrain Tags. In the last chapter, I promised to cover how to set Terrain Tags. Well, here you go.

- Make your way to the Tilesets tab of the Database.

- Find the Dungeon tileset, then click the Terrain Tag button on the right-hand side of the menu (it happens to be the last button in the list, so it should be easy to find).

- Then, find the shallow water tile and click it once. This will change its Terrain Tag from 0 to 1. See Figure 6-6 for a visual representation of the use of Terrain Tags in this exercise.

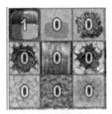

Figure 6-6. *The Water tile in the Dungeon tileset has been set to 1*

With that done, we can begin work on our common event in earnest. We'll call it CallCanoe.

```
Trigger: None
@>Control Variables: [0014:MapID] = Map ID
@>Control Variables: [0019:X] = Player's Map X
@>Control Variables: [0020:Y] = Player's Map Y
@>Conditional Branch: Player is Facing Down
  @>Control Variables: [0020:Y] += 1
  @>
```

```
: Branch End
@>Conditional Branch: Player is Facing Left
  @>Control Variables: [0020:X] -= 1
  @>
: Branch End
@>Conditional Branch: Player is Facing Right
  @>Control Variables: [0019:X] += 1
  @>
: Branch End
@>Conditional Branch: Player is Facing Up
  @>Control Variables: [0020:Y] -= 1
  @>
: Branch End
@>Get Location Info: [0013], Terrain Tag, Variable [0019][0020]
@>Conditional Branch: Variable [0013:TerrainTag] == 1
  @>Text: -, -, Normal, Bottom
  :      : You summon the canoe!
  @>Set Vehicle Location: Boat, Variable [0014][0019][0020]
  @>
: Else
  @>Text: -, -, Normal, Bottom
  :      : You can only place the canoe in shallow water!
  @>
: Branch End
@>
```

As noted before, this event is pretty easy to create. This is the event breakdown:

- We save the player's x and y coordinates and their current map ID to appropriate variables.

- Then, we alter the value of x or y, depending on the direction the player is facing. So, for example, if he/she is facing left, we reduce the value of x by 1. We do this because we want to check the square located in front of the character, and not the square it is actually on.

- After determining the x and y location of the square in front of the player character, we use **Get Location Info** to check the square's Terrain Tag.

- If the Terrain Tag is equal to 1, a text message is displayed, and the canoe is placed in front of the player. Otherwise, an error message of "You can only place the canoe in shallow water!" is returned.

■ **Note** RMVXA comes with three distinct vehicles. The Boat (which looks like a canoe) is the vehicle we are using and can only move on shallow water, hence my precautions. The Ship has sails and can move on any type of water, while the Airship looks like a blimp and can fly over any terrain but can only land on solid ground.

There you have it—a pretty cool (and easy) way for the player to have his/her own personal canoe.

■ **Note** Don't forget to use the Call Common Event Effect to add the new event to your Magic Oar item! As a reminder, you can add Effects to Items by right-clicking the Effects section and then left-clicking Edit. Call Common Event is on the Others tab of the Effect dialog menu.

The Magic Oar Chest Event

While we have worked through several different types of chests already, this particular event bears explanation, as we will handle it in an unconventional way. Before that, we want to make it so that while he exists, Kerberos blocks the player from escaping the room via Return. To do this, we can add the following snippet of code to our two Return common events.

```
@>Conditional Branch: [Magic Oar] in Inventory
  @>Conditional Branch: Switch [0013:KerberosDefeated] == OFF
    @>Text: -, -, Normal, Bottom
    :    : A malevolent presence prevents you from leaving the
    :    : room!
    @>Jump to Label: Lock
    @>
  : Branch End
  @>
: Branch End
```

■ **Note** You'll have to add a Label named Lock to the very end of the common event page. Otherwise, the player will be able to use Return, despite the message.

This makes it so that when the player opens the Magic Oar chest, he/she will be unable to escape the room unless Kerberos is defeated. Now, let's create the chest event itself.

```
@>Play SE: 'Chest', 80, 100
@>Set Move Route: This event (Wait)
 :               : $>Direction Fix OFF
 :               : $>Turn Left
 :               : $>Wait: 3 frame(s)
 :               : $>Turn Right
 :               : $>Wait: 3 frame(s)
@>Control Self Switch: A =ON
@>Fadeout Screen
@>Change Items: [Magic Oar] + 1
@>Text: -, -, Normal, Bottom
 :     : Received \C[2]Magic Oar\C[0]!
@>Text: -, -, Normal, Bottom
 :     : You have found an important item!
@>Play SE: 'Skill3', 80, 100
@>Text: -, -, Normal, Bottom
 :     : You have gained 100 EXP!
@>Change EXP: Entire Party, + 100
@>Play SE: 'Monster4', 80, 100
@>Text: -, -, Normal, Bottom
 :     : A vicious roar echoes through the area!
@>Fadein Screen
@>Text: -, -, Normal, Bottom
 :     : Kerberos has appeared! Defeat him to escape the
 :     : room!
```

In the preceding event, we cheat a little to make Kerberos's appearance more fluid. Instead of just having him suddenly pop into existence when the player grabs the Oar, we have the screen fade out before the player gets the item. Then, we go through the text as normal and award the player (and his/her companion) 100 EXP. Afterward, we play a sound effect of a monster roaring and display an appropriate text message. The screen fades in, and the player discovers that Kerberos has appeared.

■ **Note** It is possible that the player may not be strong enough to defeat Kerberos (or lack the potions needed to survive). If the player saves the game at this time, it may be rendered unwinnable. To counteract this, you can use the Change Save Access event command. Disable access to the Save menu when the player opens the Magic Oar chest and Enable it immediately before you process the Kerberos fight.

119

Kerberos, the Three-Headed Dog—Our First Boss

In Greek mythology, Kerberos (or Cerberus, if you'd rather) is the guardian of the entrance to the Underworld (a.k.a. Hades). Pretty neat, huh? Appropriately enough, this mythological dog will also guard a doorway in our game. He will appear in front of the gray door, once the player opens the chest containing the Magic Oar, and patiently await the player's presence. Here are the event pages for Kerberos, our game's first boss. You can see a screenshot of the event graphic used to represent Kerberos in Figure 6-7, immediately after the following event code.

Page 1 of 2
Condition: Item 038: Magic Oar exists
Graphic: Left-most sprite in the third row of $BigMonster1
Options: Toggle Stepping Anim. and Direction Fix
Priority: Same as Characters
Trigger: Event Touch
Contents
@>Text: -, -, Normal, Bottom
:   : Kerberos roars angrily!
@>Play SE: 'Monster4', 80, 100
@>Wait: 60 frame(s)
@>Battle Processing: Kerberos

Page 2 of 2
Condition: Switch 0013:KerberosDefeated is ON
No Graphic
No Contents

Figure 6-7. *The event graphic used to represent Kerberos on the map. This appears when the player opens the chest containing the Magic Oar*

So, when do we switch KerberosDefeated to on? During the battle, of course! The actual timing of the toggle is irrelevant, given the fact that the player cannot escape the battle. In any case, make your way to the Troops tab and find (or create, if you haven't yet) your Kerberos troop. Once you do, decide at what point in the battle you want the switch to be flipped. I'll flip it as soon as the battle starts. Here's how to add events to a Troop.

- Find the troop you wish to add event commands to.

- Look at the lower half of the dialog menu and press New Event Page (or, alternatively, edit the single page that is available by default).

- Set a condition for the event to trigger, based on what you want it to do. In this case, because I want the event to trigger at the start of the fight, I set the condition to Turn No. 0 by toggling the relevant check box in the menu that appears when you click the "..." button on the Condition bar. Turn conditions default to 0, so no additional input is required.

- Last, but not least, I set the Span to Battle so that the event only triggers once. If you set the Span to Turn, it will trigger once per turn, and if you set the Span to Moment, it will keep triggering until the condition is not met anymore (which will cause the game to hang, if the condition is always met).

With the preceding setup, all you need now is the actual event code, so here it is:

```
Condition: Turn No. 0
Span: Battle
@>Control Switches: [0013:KerberosDefeated] = ON
```

And that's all you need (yes, seriously)! When players attack and defeat Kerberos, they will once again be able to use Return and make their way around the rest of the level. More important, they will be able to use the Magic Oar to create a canoe they can board to reach the staircase leading down to the Pixies' Forest. That concludes this chapter.

■ **Note** By using the Change BGM event command, you can change the music that plays during battle. If you want to give bosses special music, that would be the command to use. Make sure you switch back to your game's default battle music after the the fight is over. If you are unclear as to how to do this, I'll cover the technicalities in Chapter 8.

Summary

During the course of this chapter, we created the Caves, our dungeon crawler's third level. We added monster encounters that trigger battles with random enemies, a lake that requires a canoe to cross, and our first boss encounter. In the next chapter, we will work on the western half of the Pixies' Forest, our dungeon's fourth level.

CHAPTER 7

■ ■ ■

The Pixies' Forest (West)

In this chapter, we will be working on our dungeon's fourth level, the western half of the Pixies' Forest. This next area will be so large that I will be splitting it into two sections, the western half and the eastern half. As such, I'll be covering this part of the game throughout the next two chapters. In this chapter, I'll be covering the western half. The canoe that the player acquired in the Caves is required to traverse this level as well, as a large part of it is flooded.

The Pixies' Forest (West)

The player character should currently be at Level 7, inching ever closer to Level 8. This, of course, means that the enemies have to be stronger, and the loot has to be better. Here are the things to cover in this chapter.

- **Ambush encounters**: The player is quietly passing through a particular area and is attacked by enemies!

- **A new town**: About the halfway point of the level, the player will find a new town, inhabited by Pixies.

- **Accessory shop**: So, the player has found two accessories already. However, there's no shop for accessories in Eagle's Crossing. We'll add one in the Pixies' town.

- **Teleporter**: We will connect the Pixies' town with Eagle's Crossing via a teleporter.

What Does the Town Greeter Have to Say?

An underground forest? You have got to be kidding me. Then again, if you found a magical oar that summons a canoe, I suppose I should stop being so incredulous. Good job on defeating that monster too, by the way. Some of the sketchier elements of our town are trying to take what they can from its corpse, but that's not my concern.

How does the town greeter know so much? Does the player's character sneak off to talk to him while the player is not playing the game? It's a mystery to everyone.

Level Overview

Make a 59×47 sized map with the Dungeon tileset, the Field4 BGM, and a GrassMaze and GrassMaze battleback. Then, see Figure 7-1 for a screenshot of the level in completed form.

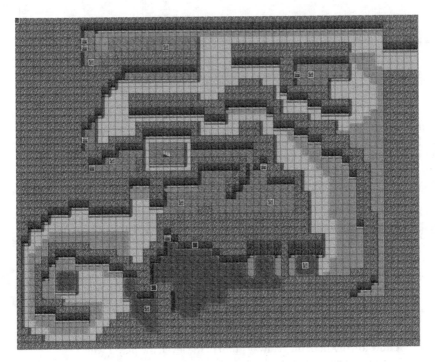

Figure 7-1. *The western half of the Pixies' Forest*

■ **Note** The tiles used to create the map are Wall (Grass Cave), Ground (Grass Cave), Water, Deep Water, and Dark Ground (Grass Maze).

The western half of the Pixies' Forest holds eight visible enemy encounters and four ambushes, as well as seven chests. The player's canoe is unable to traverse through deep water, so his/her route through the area will be somewhat constrained.

Creating Transfer Events for the Caves

By now, you should have a good idea of how to create Parallel Process transfer events. In fact, perhaps you've already created the relevant event for the Caves. In any case, because this has already become something of a habit, I might as well keep writing these down. Recall that the two exits to the Caves are located at 016,018 and 061,041.

```
Trigger: Parallel Process
@>Control Variables: [0019:X] = Player's Map X
@>Control Variables: [0020:Y] = Player's Map Y
@>Conditional Branch: Variable [0019:X] == 16
  @>Conditional Branch: Variable [0020:Y] == 18
    @>Conditional Branch: Self Switch B == OFF
      @>Control Variables: [0001:DeepestDungeonFloor] = 4
      @>Control Self Switch: B =ON
      @>Transfer Player:[010:Level 4] (023,019), Right
    : Else
      @>Transfer Player:[010:Level 4] (023,019), Right
      @>
    : Branch End
    @>
  : Branch End
  @>
: Branch End
@>Conditional Branch: Variable [0019:X] == 61
  @>Conditional Branch: Variable [0020:Y] == 41
    @>Transfer Player:[007:Level 2] (055,043), Down
    @>
  : Branch End
  @>
: Branch End
@>
```

The Enemies of the Pixies' Forest (West)

We have tread a lot of ground in terms of different types of enemy encounters. For this dungeon level, we will add four ambush encounters that appear when the player crosses certain areas of the water. I'll cover those encounters in a later section. For now, see Table 7-1 for a list of enemy encounters in the Pixies' Forest (West).

Table 7-1. *List of the Enemies the Player Will Face in the Western Part of the Pixies' Forest*

Name	MHP	MMP	ATK	DEF	MAT	MDF	AGI	LUK	HIT%	EVA%	Attack Element
Cockatrice	36	0	16	8	1	1	6	6	90	10	Pierce
Gargoyle	40	24	12	12	7	7	2	10	85	0	Crush
Man-Eating Plant	40	15	18	6	1	1	1	10	85	5	Slash

Because the player has officially passed the halfway point of the game, the enemies will be offering more experience and gold than ever before. Table 7-2 will provide the item drop list and skill list for our three enemies.

Table 7-2. *Item Drops and Skills for the Enemies in the Western Half of Pixies' Forest*

Name	EXP	G	Item Drop Slot 1 (Drop Chance)	Item Drop Slot 2 (Drop Chance)	Item Drop Slot 3 (Drop Chance)	Skill List (Rating)
Cockatrice	36	54	Antidote (1/4)	Para-Cure (1/10)	None	Poison Bite (5), Trip (4), Glare (4)
Gargoyle	40	58	Lesser Restoration Potion (1/4)	Scroll of Chill (1/20)	None	Attack (5), Chill (5)
Man-Eating Plant	45	60	Smelling Salts (1/5)	Scroll of Sleep (1/10)	None	Attack (5), Sleep (5), Poison Cloud (4)

The Man-Eating Plant takes double damage from Slash-based attacks and half-damage from Crush-based attacks but is immune to the Sleep State. You can use the State Rate Feature to set an enemy's resistance to a particular State. Setting the rate to 0% grants them immunity. The Gargoyle enemy is immune to Poison. See Table 7-3 for a breakdown of the new skills created for this chapter.

Table 7-3. *List of New Skills Created for This Dungeon Level*

Skill Name	Element	Description	Damage Formula	Notes
Trip	Crush	Attempts to trip an enemy	a.atk > b.def ? a.atk - b.def : 1	Used by Cockatrices. Has a 70% success rate (as defined in the Invocations section) and inflicts the Stun state if it connects
Glare	None	May paralyze an enemy	None	Used by Cockatrices. Has a 50% chance of inflicting Paralysis on the target

---

■ **Note** The preceding can be accomplished with State Resist, but you should never give an enemy a State Resist to Death. While our game will not have such an effect, if you wish to include an instant death effect to which enemies are immune, give the enemies a State Rate of 0% to Death instead.

The only enemy in this dungeon level that has new skills is the Cockatrice. While the Cockatrice is known for petrifying its victims, such an effect would be a bit excessive for our game. Instead, let's just give it a paralysis effect. The player should have a companion by this point, and this particular monster is a case study in why. The player will have a hard time doing anything if he/she gets stunned and/or paralyzed repeatedly and has no help. Now, let's cover the concept of enemy ambushes and how we create them in RPG Maker VX Ace (RMVXA).

Ambush Encounters

In role-playing games (RPGs), the most common types of encounters are usually random (enemies that attack the player after a certain average number of steps) or static. During the course of creating our dungeon crawler, we have been incorporating various types of visible static encounters. Now, I'm going to create some encounters that trigger when the player passes through a certain area. How do we accomplish this? The easiest way is via Terrain Tags or regions. Given the fact that I'm going to place the encounters in the water, and we are already using Terrain Tags for the canoe common event logic, I will be using regions instead. Figure 7-2 is a screenshot of the dungeon level in Region Mode, which shows the four ambush locations.

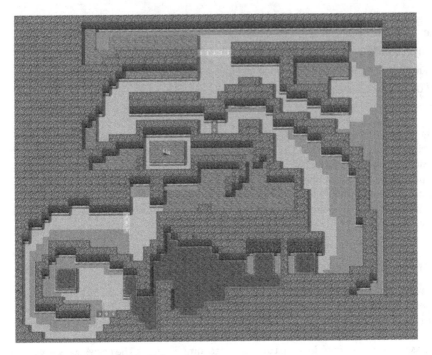

Figure 7-2. *The four ambush locations*

■ **Note** Adding regions to a map is as easy as using Region Editing Mode. You can access it from the Mode option on the menu toolbar or by pressing F7.

For the sake of clarity in black-and-white versions of this text, I used Regions 3 and 9 to draw the four ambush locations. However, as you'll see in the next section, the regions actually used for the ambush code are 1 through 4. Here's a list of exactly where you have to draw each individual region on the map. (You can refer to the appropriate map in the download package to verify these exact locations.)

- **Region 1:** (016,028), (016,029), and (016,030)

- **Region 2:** (012,042), (013,042), and (014,042)

- **Region 3:** (029,015) and (029,016)

- **Region 4:** (027,005), (028,005), (029,005), (030,005), and (031,005)

The Ambush Encounter Parallel Process Event

We will be using a Parallel Process event, in conjunction with self-switches, to handle the ambush encounters. Here is the full event:

```
Trigger: Parallel Process
@>Control Variables: [0019:X] = Player's Map X
@>Control Variables: [0020:Y] = Player's Map Y
@>Get Location Info: [0018], Region ID, Variable [0019][0020]
@>Conditional Branch: Variable [0018:Region] == 1
  @>Conditional Branch: Self Switch A == OFF
    @>Text: -, -, Normal, Bottom
    :     : Ambush!
    @>Battle Processing: Cockatrice
    @>Control Self Switch: A =ON
    @>
  : Branch End
  @>
: Branch End
@>Conditional Branch: Variable [0018:Region] == 2
  @>Conditional Branch: Self Switch B == OFF
    @>Text: -, -, Normal, Bottom
    :     : Ambush!
    @>Battle Processing: Gargoyle
    @>Control Self Switch: B =ON
    @>
  : Branch End
  @>
: Branch End
@>Conditional Branch: Variable [0018:Region] == 3
  @>Conditional Branch: Self Switch C == OFF
    @>Text: -, -, Normal, Bottom
    :     : Ambush!
    @>Battle Processing: Cockatrice*2
    @>Control Self Switch: C =ON
    @>
  : Branch End
  @>
: Branch End
@>Conditional Branch: Variable [0018:Region] == 4
  @>Conditional Branch: Self Switch D == OFF
    @>Text: -, -, Normal, Bottom
    :     : Ambush!
    @>Battle Processing: Gargoyle*2
    @>Control Self Switch: D =ON
    @>
```

```
  : Branch End
  @>
: Branch End
```

The general idea of this event is the following: the first time the player sails into an ambush point, he/she will be forced to fight one (first two ambushes) or two (second two ambushes) enemies. The player cannot escape the battles, but these do not re-spawn in the way that most other enemy encounter events do.

■ **Note** I created four ambushes for the sake of efficiency, as each event has four self-switches it can use. If you want more ambushes, you have to use extra switches.

As is proper, the ambushes get harder and harder as the player progresses through the area.

Unlocking the Pixies' Vale

The player has gotten through three levels of the game's dungeon and is continually approaching the game's final objective. However, while using Return Crystals (or the Return spell) provides a way to instantly return to town when needed, it would still be nice to have an actual teleport spot. The perfect place to put it is within another town. That way, we can connect both towns. The Pixies' town is hidden from mortal sight behind some otherwise inconspicuous vines (at 026,032) some ways to the south of the staircase leading back to the previous level. However, attempts to reach the vines that lead into the town will fail, as a barrier of vines to the south will stop the player from getting that far. The way forward lies with a lone Pixie, exiled to a small island to the west of her home. See Figure 7-3 for a screenshot of the area surrounding the entrance to the Pixies' Vale.

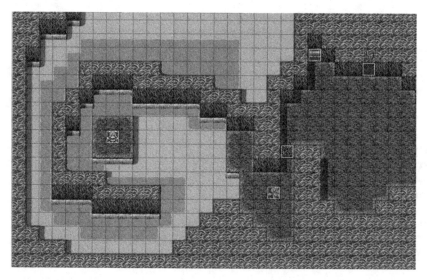

Figure 7-3. *The entrance to the Pixies' Vale is to the east of the treasure chest*

The player will have to speak to the Pixie on the island to receive her help. If the player interacts with the vines before talking to the Pixie, she will call them to her side. In either case, she will "join" (in a guest capacity, not as an actual party member) the player and allow him/her to progress. See Figure 7-4 for the Pixie's graphic, then keep on reading to see her event code.

Figure 7-4. *The graphic I use for this Pixie (and all other Pixies, save the Queen). You can find this graphic within the Spiritual graphic set*

Page 1 of 2
Graphic: See Figure 7-4
Priority: Same as Characters
Trigger: Action Button
Contents
@>Text: -, -, Normal, Bottom
   :   : Hello! If you wish to get past the vines, I can help
   :   : you. Please take me with you!

```
@>Text: -, -, Normal, Bottom
:     : The Pixie forces herself into your party.
@>Fadeout Screen
@>Wait: 30 frame(s)
@>Control Switches: [0014:PixieJoin] = ON
@>Fadein Screen
@>
```

Page 2 of 2
Priority: Below Characters
Trigger: Action Button
No Graphic
No Contents

Once the player has the Pixie in his/her party, interacting with the vines blocking the way to the rest of the level will allow her to take them down. On that note, see Figure 7-5 to see the Wall Vine graphic to be used for this event and then read on to see the event code.

Figure 7-5. *The lower half of the Wall Vine graphic in Dungeon's tileset-B sprite set*

Page 1 of 3
Graphic: See Figure 7-5
Options: Toggle Direction Fix
Priority: Same as Characters
Trigger: Action Button
Contents
```
@>Text: -, -, Normal, Bottom
:     : You see a wall of brambles.
@>Text: -, -, Normal, Bottom
:     : A melodic voice sounds from the west.
@>Text: -, -, Normal, Bottom
:     : Come over here. I can open that for you.
@>
```

Page 2 of 3
Condition: 0014:PixieJoin is ON
Graphic: See Figure 7-5
Options: Toggle Direction Fix

Priority: Same as Characters
Trigger: Action Button
@>Text: -, -, Normal, Bottom
:   : You see a wall of brambles.
@>Text: -, -, Normal, Bottom
:   : The Pixie places a hand on the brambles and they
:   : recede into the grassy wall!
@>Fadeout Screen
@>Control Self Switch: A =ON
@>Wait: 30 frame(s)
@>Fadein Screen
@>Text: -, -, Normal, Bottom
:   : We should visit my queen. She would be happy to
:   : see someone such as yourself. Our town is hidden
:   : behind those solitary vines.

Page 3 of 3
Condition: Self Switch A is ON
Priority: Below Characters
Trigger: Action Button
No Graphic
No Contents

With the help of a mystical fairy creature, the player is within a few paces of the entrance to the Pixie's Vale. That, of course, means that we have to create the town as well. The Pixies' Vale, much like Eagle's Crossing, is actually a pair of maps. The first map is the town exterior; the second map is the town interior. Unlike Eagle's Crossing, the interiors of each building are directly connected to one another. Anyway, when the player interacts with the wall vines that hide the entrance to the Pixies' Vale, the Pixie will brush her hand against the vines, and the player will be transferred appropriately. Here's the event in question, which is a single page in length:

Graphic: None
Priority: Same as Characters
Trigger: Action Button
@>Text: -, -, Normal, Bottom
:   : You see some vines clinging to the wall.
@>Text: -, -, Normal, Bottom
:   : The Pixie sticks out her hand and brushes the vines,
@>Transfer Player:[011:Pixies' Vale] (012,004), Down
@>

■ **Note**   You can use the lower half of the Wall Vine graphic for the event and then draw only the top half, using Map Mode, instead of drawing both halves of the graphic and having a blank event graphic. Either method is fine.

The obvious question now would be, what does the Pixies' Vale look like? It's a 25×25 map that uses the Exterior tileset and (among other tiles) the Forest tile for its buildings. Take a look at Figure 7-6.

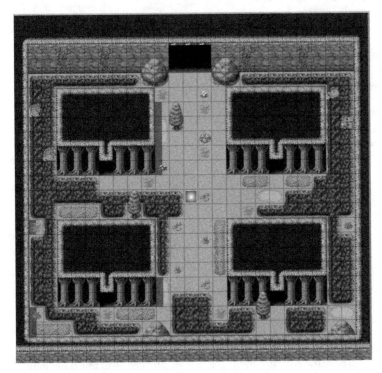

Figure 7-6. *The Pixies' Vale. Note the similarities in layout with Eagle's Crossing*

You may have already noticed a graphic in the center of the town that looks identical to the Return portal in Eagle's Crossing. We'll touch upon that soon.

The Queen of the Pixies

The player now finds him-/herself within a natural village, with buildings made out of the very trees of a forest and interiors that wind into the belly of the earth. The player seeks the queen of the Pixies. Luckily, she's as close as entering any one of the three accessible natural buildings (the southeastern building cannot be reached from the outside). Here is the Parallel Process transfer event I use for the various exits in the Pixies' Vale.

Trigger: Parallel Process
@>Control Variables: [0019:X] = Player's Map X
@>Control Variables: [0020:Y] = Player's Map Y
@>Conditional Branch: Variable [0020:Y] == 3

```
@>Transfer Player:[010:Level 4] (026,033), Down
  @>
: Branch End
@>Conditional Branch: Variable [0019:X] == 6
  @>Conditional Branch: Variable [0020:Y] == 10
    @>Transfer Player:[012:Interior] (007,005), Down
    @>
  : Branch End
  @>
: Branch End
@>Conditional Branch: Variable [0019:X] == 18
  @>Conditional Branch: Variable [0020:Y] == 10
    @>Transfer Player:[012:Interior] (017,005), Down
    @>
  : Branch End
  @>
: Branch End
@>Conditional Branch: Variable [0019:X] == 6
  @>Conditional Branch: Variable [0020:Y] == 19
    @>Transfer Player:[012:Interior] (007,020), Down
    @>
  : Branch End
  @>
: Branch End
@>Conditional Branch: Variable [0019:X] == 18
  @>Conditional Branch: Variable [0020:Y] == 19
    @>Transfer Player:[012:Interior] (017,020), Down
    @>
  : Branch End
  @>
: Branch End
@>
```

As usual, place that event somewhere the player cannot normally reach, just to be safe. Then, see Figure 7-7 for a picture of the interior map for the Pixies' Vale.

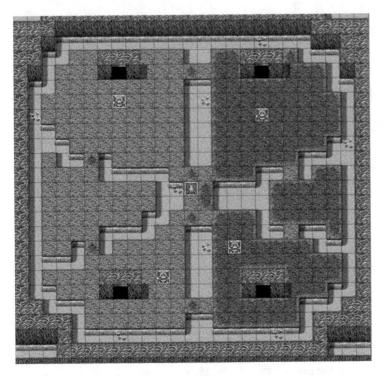

Figure 7-7. *The interior of the Pixies' Vale*

■ **Note**   Given that finding the Vale advances the main story, I would give the player some story experience here. I personally give the player 500 EXP via an Autorun event that triggers the first time the player enters the Pixies' Vale. This helps to compensate a bit for the otherwise lackluster experience gains that this level offers.

Once inside, the player will see four pixies surrounding a green-haired character in the middle. That is Titania, the Queen of the Pixies. (Neat trivia fact: It was William Shakespeare who, in *A Midsummer Night's Dream*, originally bestowed a name on the queen of the fairies. In popular folklore, she had no actual name until then.) Each of the four pixies are two-page events. The first page is identical for all four of the pixies. The code is as follows.

Priority: Same as Characters
Trigger: Action Button
@>Text: -, -, Normal, Bottom
:   : A human...here? Please, talk to our queen.

For the second page, each of the Pixies will be different. I will provide a bullet list of what has to be spread among the Pixies, with the only caveat being that the very first bullet must be the southeastern Pixie's second page, for reasons that will soon become apparent. First, here are the settings that should be identical for the four second pages:

Condition: 0015: QueenTalk is ON
Priority: Same as Characters
Trigger: Action Button

With that out of the way, here's the bullet list.

- If you take the stairs next to me, you'll find our town's shopkeeper. She deals in rare amulets and accessories that you might find use for.

- We used to live above ground in times long past. However, we fled into secrecy when humans started to expand their society.

- We have lived within this vale for centuries. Once, we were more. Someday, we will be gone.

- The remaining Pixie should function as an inn, allowing the player to rest for free.

The QueenTalk switch will be flipped on when the player speaks with Titania. See Figure 7-8 for the graphic used for our Pixie queen.

Figure 7-8. The graphic used for our Queen of the Pixies. You can find this one in the Spiritual graphic set, much like the other we used for the Pixies

Titania's event will have three pages. The first page is, for lack of a better term, an info dump. The player receives a lot of information concerning the happenings in the area and receives his/her next objective: to destroy a monster called Lamia. Without further ado, see the following for page 1 of Titania's event.

Page 1 of 3
Graphic: See Figure 7-8
Priority: Same as Characters
Trigger: Action Button
@>Text: -, -, Normal, Bottom
:   : It has been far too long since we had last seen a

```
   :      : human. My name is Titania, and I am the queen of
   :      : the Pixies.
@>Text: -, -, Normal, Bottom
   :      : Your Pixie companion pops into existence as the
   :      : Queen frowns.
@>Text: -, -, Normal, Bottom
   :      : That explains how you were able to enter the Vale.
   :      : Yet, now is not the time for reprimands. Instead,
   :      : I would ask for your help and entrust that Pixie
   :      : to you.
@>Text: -, -, Normal, Bottom
   :      : The Queen looks at your Pixie companion.
@>Text: -, -, Normal, Bottom
   :      : Astala, you will accompany this human.
@>Text: -, -, Normal, Bottom
   :      : The Pixie meekishly nods.
@>Text: -, -, Normal, Bottom
   :      : Good. I had exiled Astala for releasing the monster
   :      : Lamia from her prison atop the Ancient Temple. She
   :      : gave heed to the monster's lies and imperiled us
   :      : all.
@>Text: -, -, Normal, Bottom
   :      : Lamia has already corrupted some of my brethren,
   :      : turning them into ghastly aberrations of their
   :      : former selves.
@>Text: -, -, Normal, Bottom
   :      : Astala can open the way for you. You need only find
   :      : \C[2]the center of a group of wall vines\C[0] to make your way
   :      : deeper into the forest. You may also find other
   :      : secrets within vines farther in the forest as well.
@>Text: -, -, Normal, Bottom
   :      : Titania closes her eyes for a few seconds and then
   :      : opens them.
@>Text: -, -, Normal, Bottom
   :      : I have activated the portal that connects our city
   :      : with the human town of Eagle's Crossing.
@>Text: -, -, Normal, Bottom
   :      : You'll find the portal outside.
@>Text: -, -, Normal, Bottom
   :      : Please make your way back here once you have
   :      : defeated Lamia.
@>Control Switches: [0015:QueenTalk] = ON
```

Titania reveals the name of the Pixie accompanying the player character and then drops a hint about secrets hidden within vines deeper in the forest. I highlight this within the text via the use of one of RMVXA's various text modifiers. Writing \C[n] (where n is a number; in the preceding event code, 2 is orange and 0 is white) changes the color of the text that follows the modifier. For the player, learning about the vines and the secrets they hold will be particularly important in the next chapter, when he/she visits the eastern half of the Pixies' Forest. Once the queen has finished speaking, the QueenTalk switch is flipped, and the portal in the town exterior is activated. Talking to the queen again after this sequence but before defeating Lamia reveals the second page of her event.

Page 2 of 3
Condition: 0015: QueenTalk is ON
Graphic: Same as Page 1 of the event
Priority: Same as Characters
Trigger: Action Button
@>Text: -, -, Normal, Bottom
:   : I sense that Lamia still lives. I must concentrate
:   : on suppressing her power. Please leave me be.

In a nutshell, the second page of Titania's event is a not-so-subtle nudge to the player to continue the game, rather than stick around. I will discuss the last page of this event in the next chapter. For now, there are two more events within the Pixies' Vale.

The Accessory Shop

You'll recall that, in the exterior part of the Pixies' Vale, the southeastern building is inaccessible. The player must make his/her way into the interior and then take the southeastern exit back to the exterior. If the player has spoken with Titania, he/she will find a solitary Pixie floating directly below the nearby tree. She is this game's accessory shop. The event in question is a single page in size and requires that QueenTalk be on, using the same graphic as we used for the other Pixies so far. The player can talk with the Pixie to receive a warm welcome and shop for accessories. As we have made several shops already, I'll gloss over the event and, instead, list some new accessories in Table 7-4 that should be included in the shop's lineup. You should be able to create all of these items, using the skills you've learned so far in this book.

Table 7-4. The New Accessories to Be Created for the Accessory Shop

Name	Description	Price
Magic Amulet	Increases the wearer's MAT by 5 and MMP by 10	2500 G
Fury Amulet	Increases the wearer's ATK by 10	3000 G
Truestrike Amulet	Increases the wearer's ATK by 5 and HIT by 10%	3000 G
Shield Amulet	Increases the wearer's DEF and MDF by 10	5000 G
Mystic Amulet	Increases the wearer's MAT by 10 and MMP by 20	7500 G
Cloak of Evasion	Increases the wearer's EVA by 35%	5000 G
Haste Plume	Increases the wearer's AGI by 10	3000 G
Anti-Crush	A mysterious trinket that halves Crush-based damage	2500 G
Anti-Slash	A mysterious trinket that halves Slash-based damage	2500 G
Anti-Pierce	A mysterious trinket that halves Pierce-based damage	2500 G

Including the four accessories we created in the previous chapter, our game now has a total of eleven accessories for the player to acquire.

The Portal to Eagle's Crossing

The portal leading back to Eagle's Crossing opens once QueenTalk is on, much like the Accessory Shop. Once it is open, the player can stand on it and press the Action button to receive a prompt asking him/her if he/she wishes to travel to Eagle's Crossing. If the player says yes, he/she will appear in front of the vines behind the Equipment Shop in Eagle's Crossing. The portal event is one page long and consists of the following code:

```
Condition: 0015: QueenTalk is ON
Priority: Below Characters
Trigger: Action Button
@>Text: -, -, Normal, Bottom
:     : You see a portal leading back to the surface.
:     : Will you use the portal?
@>Show Choices: Yes, No
: When [Yes]
  @>Control Switches: [0009:InTown] = ON
  @>Transfer Player:[001:Eagle's Crossing] (005,004), Down
  @>
: When [No]
  @>
: Branch End
@>
```

Figure 7-9 is a screenshot of the portal graphic located in !Flame (which you should recognize as the graphic used for the Return portal back in Chapter 4).

Figure 7-9. The graphic we will be using for our Pixies' Vale portal

When the player takes the portal back to Eagle's Crossing, he/she will appear in the location displayed in Figure 7-10.

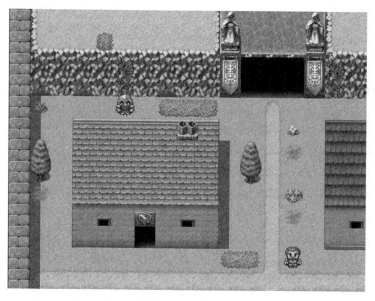

Figure 7-10. In-game screenshot of Palnor immediately after using the portal at the Pixies' Vale

Of course, a portal isn't much good if it's only one-way, so let's add an event to that wall vine behind Palnor, so that the player can get back to Pixies' Vale.

Condition: 0015:QueenTalk is ON
Priority: Same as Characters
Trigger: Action Button
@>Text: -, -, Normal, Bottom
:　　: You see a portal to the Pixies' Vale cleverly hidden

141

```
:       : in between the vines. Will you use it?
@>Show Choices: Yes, No
: When [Yes]
  @>Control Switches: [0009:InTown] = OFF
  @>Transfer Player:[011:Pixies' Vale] (012,012), Down
  @>
: When [No]
  @>
: Branch End
@>
```

■ **Note**   I use that specific conditional on the event, as it would not make much sense to allow the player to skip through half of the game by finding the portal early. That is without even mentioning the logical flaw that would surface, given that Titania does not open the portal until the player talks to her.

With all of that said, we are done with the Pixies' Vale.

The Treasure of Pixies' Forest (West)

There are a total of seven treasure chests in this dungeon level, divided into three types of loot tables. Here are their contents, and you can place them wherever you like in the level.

1. Character-specific treasure (Palnor/Gust/Feylia)

   - Steel Sword/Steel Bow/1500 Gold

   - Steel Chestplate/Steel Chestplate/Cloak of Evasion

2. Random treasure

   - Panacea (60%)/Gold Nugget (40%)

   - Lesser Restoration Potion (80%)/Restoration Potion (20%)

3. Normal treasure

   - Return Crystal

   - 1000 Gold

   - Phoenix Tears

As usual, I prefer to place the most valuable treasure chests in the places hardest to reach.

The Path to Pixies' Forest (East)

To close out this chapter, I'm going to display two more locations that require transfer events. The first one is located directly to the east of the vines that lead into the Pixies' Vale. Interacting with those vines will take the player to a similar set not more than a few squares further east, *if* he/she has already talked to Titania. Otherwise, the vines will do nothing. See Figure 7-11 for a view of the area I am referring to.

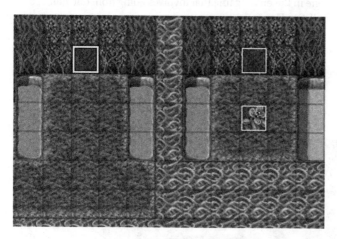

Figure 7-11. *The location to the east of the entrance of the Vale. Note the transfer events in the center of both sets of vines*

The transfer events are located at 036,033 and 042,033, respectively. Here's the relevant event code for both:

Event at 036,033
Condition: Switch 0015:QueenTalk is ON
Priority: Same as Characters
Trigger: Action Button
@>Play SE: 'Move', 80, 100
@>Transfer Player:[010:Level 4] (042,034), Down
@>

Event at 042,033
Condition: Switch 0015:QueenTalk is ON
Priority: Same as Characters
Trigger: Action Button
@>Play SE: 'Move', 80, 100
@>Transfer Player:[010:Level 4] (036,034), Down
@>

■ **Note**   This is one case where the event priority is important. If the priority of these particular transfer events is not Same as Characters, the player will not be able to interact with them.

The other location is the place where we should connect this level to the fifth dungeon level (which we'll officially do in the next chapter). This particular transition is notable in that it is the only one in the entire game that involves going from one half of a dungeon level to the other half. See Figure 7-12.

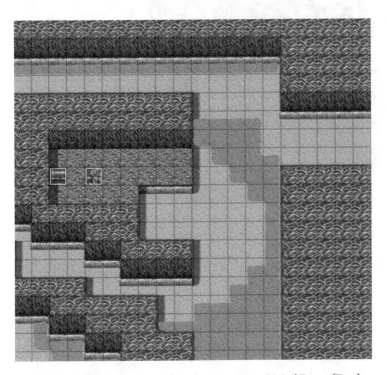

Figure 7-12.   *The area surrounding the entrance to Pixies' Forest (East)*

Once the player reaches the gap in the grass wall on the far right side of the area, he/she will pass into the eastern half of the level. That, howeve, is the subject of the next chapter.

Summary

During the course of this chapter, we created the western half of the Pixies' Forest, our dungeon crawler's fourth level. We added monster encounters that are triggered when the player passes through a specific area, a secret town inhabited by Pixies, and a quest that requires the player to travel to the next level to complete. In the next chapter, we will work on the eastern half of the Pixies' Forest, our dungeon's penultimate level.

■ ■ ■

CHAPTER 8

The Pixies' Forest (East)

In this chapter, we will be working on our dungeon's fifth level, the eastern half of the Pixies' Forest. The player is close to finishing the game and will fight his/her last boss at the end of this particular area (as the Ancient Temple won't have an actual boss). The canoe that the player received in the Caves will be upgraded here, so that the player can progress, given that most of the level is made up of deep water.

The Pixies' Forest (East)

With the experience provided by the game so far, the player character should currently be at Level 11 (within about 200 experience points from reaching Level 12). Here are the things I'll cover in this chapter:

- **Hidden dwellings**: The player was advised, by his/her Pixie companion, of the way to find hidden places within the forest. This level will have several of those. Some will advance the player's progress, while others will lead to locations hiding a single Pixie that will impart some information.

- **An upgradable item**: As already noted in the chapter's introduction, the player's canoe is ill equipped for this level, given the amount of deep water that it contains. We will create a nonplayer character (NPC) that swaps the player's Magic Oar for a Magic Sail.

- **The final boss**: Lamia stands atop the ruins of the Ancient Temple and must be defeated, so that Titania will be able to send the player to the game's final level.

What Does the Town Greeter Have to Say?

> *The forest goes deeper? I'm not even sure what to say anymore. Could the ancient artifact be somewhere inside that forest?*

The answer to that is both yes *and* no, not that the town greeter would care much about the difference.

Level Overview

Much like in the previous chapter, you'll want to make a 59×47 sized map with the Dungeon tileset, the Field4 BGM, and a GrassMaze and GrassMaze battleback. Afterward, see Figure 8-1 for a screenshot of the level in completed form.

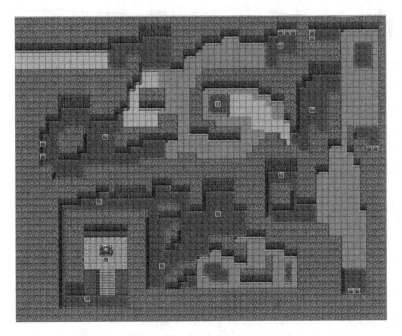

Figure 8-1. *The eastern half of the Pixies' Forest*

■ **Note**   The tiles used to create the map are the same as in Chapter 7: Wall (Grass Cave), Ground (Grass Cave), Water, Deep Water, and Dark Ground (Grass Maze).

The eastern half of the Pixies' Forest contains eight visible enemy encounters and eleven chests. The player's boat cannot sail through deep water, so his/her first order of business will be to find the Magic Sail that will upgrade his/her Magic Oar. As is standard by now, let's start the chapter by talking about transfer events.

Creating Transfer Events for the Pixies' Forest

You may be surprised to know that this will be the last time that I include such a section in a chapter. We must add the Parallel Process transfer event to cover both exits of the western part of the forest and then add another one in the eastern part for the way back to the previous level. First, let's create the event for the previous level. The exits are at 022,019, and the three squares at 058X with y coordinates of 5, 6, and 7, respectively.

```
Trigger: Parallel Process
@>Control Variables: [0019:X] = Player's Map X
@>Control Variables: [0020:Y] = Player's Map Y
@>Conditional Branch: Variable [0019:X] == 58
  @>Conditional Branch: Self Switch B == OFF
    @>Control Variables: [0001:DeepestDungeonFloor] = 5
    @>Control Self Switch: B =ON
    @>Transfer Player:[013:Level 5] (001,006), Right
  : Else
    @>Transfer Player:[013:Level 5] (001,006), Right
    @>
  : Branch End
  @>
: Branch End
@>Conditional Branch: Variable [0019:X] == 22
  @>Conditional Branch: Variable [0020:Y] == 19
    @>Transfer Player:[009:Level 3] (016,019), Down
    @>
  : Branch End
  @>
: Branch End
@>
```

Now, switch over to our current dungeon level to make the transfer event that leads back to the previous level. The exit is located at 000X.

```
Trigger: Parallel Process
@>Control Variables: [0019:X] = Player's Map X
@>Control Variables: [0020:Y] = Player's Map Y
@>Conditional Branch: Variable [0019:X] == 0
  @>Transfer Player:[010:Level 4] (057,006), Left
  @>
: Branch End
@>
```

We need only one more transfer event in this game, and it will be covered at the end of this chapter. You're almost done with the game. Keep it up!

The Enemies of the Pixies' Forest (East)

The penultimate level of the game will have encounters in the form of enemy pairs. So, when the player runs into an enemy sprite, he/she will be attacked by two units of that enemy (the obvious exception, of course, being the level boss). See Table 8-1 for the list of enemies.

Table 8-1. *List of Enemies the Player Will Face in the Eastern Part of the Pixies' Forest*

Name	MHP	MMP	ATK	DEF	MAT	MDF	AGI	LUK	HIT%	EVA%	Attack Element
Orc	45	0	18	9	1	1	5	5	90	5	Slash
Sahagin	52	36	20	10	10	5	4	8	95	5	Pierce
Lamia	200	200	24	14	14	7	10	10	100	5	Crush

Lamia is the game's final boss and serves as one last roadblock to the player's gaining entry to the Ancient Temple. Orcs and Sahagins form the normal enemy encounters, and they will do their best to stop the player as he/she tries to make his/her way to Lamia. See Table 8-2 for additional details concerning the enemies.

Table 8-2. *Rewards and Skills for the Enemies in the Eastern Half of Pixies' Forest*

Name	EXP	G	Item Drop Slot 1 (Drop Chance)	Item Drop Slot 2 (Drop Chance)	Item Drop Slot 3 (Drop Chance)	Skill List (Rating; Comments)
Orc	60	75	Mythril Axe (1/20)	Scroll of Immolate (1/20)	None	Attack (5), Rage (10; used on turn 1 and every five turns thereafter), Cleave (5)
Sahagin	65	80	Mythril Dagger (1/20)	Scroll of Blizzard (1/20)	None	Puncture (10; used on turn 1 and every four turns thereafter), Attack (5), Chill (5), Poison Fang (5)
Lamia	500	625	Lamia's Hide (1/1)	None	None	Attack (4), Rend (4), Rage (10; used on turn 1 and every five turns thereafter), Trip (7; used on turn 3 and every three turns thereafter), Blizzard (5; added to action patterns when Lamia is at 50% HP or lower)

As befitting a boss, Lamia has a more complex attack pattern than the standard enemies. While most of the skills used for the new enemies were created in earlier chapters, there are three new skills to note. Take a look at Table 8-3 for details.

Table 8-3. *List of New Skills Created for This Dungeon Level*

Skill Name	Element	Description	Damage Formula	Notes
Cleave	Slash	A sweeping strike that ignores armor	`a.atk`	Used by Orcs. Hits all enemies. Since it does damage equal to the user's a.atk, it would do 18 damage when used by an Orc and 27 by an Orc affected by Rage.
Puncture	Pierce	Damages the enemy and lowers its DEF by 50% for 4 turns	None	Used by Sahagin. The DEF debuff is applied via two uses of the Add Debuff: DEF Effect.
Rage	None	Increases user's ATK by 50% for 5 turns	None	Used by Orcs and Lamia. The ATK boost is applied via two instances of the Add Buff: ATK Effect.

As you can see, all of the new skills involve improving the enemy's ability to inflict physical damage or reduce the player character's ability to withstand it. As play-testing should bear out, Palnor's high HP and DEF make him nearly impossible to defeat by most enemies, unless the player is careless about keeping his/her HP topped off. These monsters should do quite a bit to force the player to be more proactive in dungeon battles, instead of merely being able to select Attack to win every single fight.

■ **Note** Having an easy character is not necessarily bad in a game that offers choices. The player can decide to challenge him-/herself in a subsequent run by playing as Gust or Feylia.

Paired Encounters

There's not much else to say about the usual enemy encounters themselves, given the fact that the eventing doesn't particularly deviate from what has been discussed up to now. Without further ado, look below for the relevant event code for the Sahagin encounters.

```
@>Battle Processing: Sahagin*2
: If Win
  @>Erase Event
  @>
: If Escape
  @>Set Move Route: This event
  :                    : $>Wait: 300 frame(s)
  @>
: Branch End
@>
```

For the Orc encounters, you need only replace the Battle Processing event with a troop of 2 Orcs instead of 2 Sahagins. I'll cover the Lamia encounter later in the chapter.

Hidden Dwellings and Portals

When players first make their way to the eastern side of the Pixies' Forest, they will find that they are only able to traverse an extremely limited portion of the area. There are several locations of interest that lead to hidden locations or connect to another part of the dungeon level. A player can access them by interacting with the middle vine in a group of five wall vines. See Figure 8-2 for a screenshot marking each of the various wall vines.

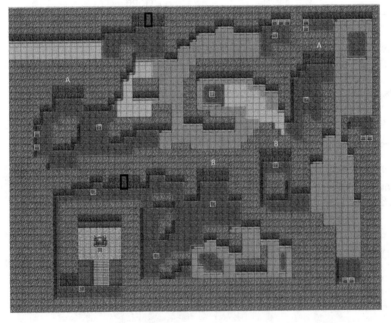

Figure 8-2. The eastern half of the Pixies' Forest, with added markings

As you can see in Figure 8-2, there are two rectangles that denote hidden dwellings and two pairs of letters that denote teleporters. The player will want to go through the *A* portal on the left side of the area, which will take him/her to the other side of the level, where he/she can call his/her canoe to reach a solitary island not unlike the one where his/her Pixie companion was found.

The Magic Sail

The Pixie on that solitary island at 032,013 will turn the player's Magic Oar into a Magic Sail. Here's the relevant event code for the Pixie.

```
@>Text: -, -, Normal, Bottom
:      : Hello!
@>Text: -, -, Normal, Bottom
:      : The Pixie looks at you intently for a few seconds.
@>Text: -, -, Normal, Bottom
:      : I feel the presence of a \C[2]Magic Oar\C[0]. If you give it
:      : to me, I can turn it into a \C[2]Magic Sail\C[0]. That will
:      : allow you to call forth a ship that can travel in
:      : \C[18]deep water\C[0].
@>Text: -, -, Normal, Bottom
:      : Will you give the Magic Oar to the Pixie?
@>Show Choices: Yes, No
: When [Yes]
  @>Text: -, -, Normal, Bottom
  :      : You hand over the \C[2]Magic Oar\C[0] to the Pixie.
  @>Text: -, -, Normal, Bottom
  :      : The Pixie closes her eyes and utters a few words of
  :      : magic.
  @>Flash Screen: (255,255,255,255), @60, Wait
  @>Text: -, -, Normal, Bottom
  :      : Here, that should do it.
  @>Play ME: 'Fanfare1', 100, 100
  @>Text: -, -, Normal, Bottom
  :      : The \C[2]Magic Oar\C[0] has become the \C[2]Magic Sail\C[0]!
  @>Change Items: [Magic Oar], - 1
  @>Change Items: [Magic Sail], + 1
  @>Text: -, -, Normal, Bottom
  :      : Stay safe!
  @>Fadeout Screen
  @>Set Vehicle Location: Boat, [006:Dungeon] (008,010)
  @>Wait: 30 frame(s)
  @>Fadein Screen
  @>Control Self Switch: A =ON
  @>
```

```
: When [No]
  @>
: Branch End
@>
```

■ **Note**   The previous event does not check to see if the player actually has the Magic Oar in his/her inventory. Keep in mind that it is impossible for the player to reach the Pixie without the aid of the Magic Oar. Still, checking to see if the item is in the player's inventory is as easy as using a Conditional Branch.

Note how we remove the Magic Oar from the player's inventory and add the Magic Sail in its place. Additionally, because the player won't be using the Boat anymore, we use a Set Vehicle Location event command (along with a Fadein/Fadeout to hide the actual vehicle transfer) to send it off to the character select map (as the player doesn't set foot in there after a character has been chosen). Of course, the Magic Sail is going to be of little use to the player unless we associate a common event to it. For this purpose, we can copy the Magic Oar common event and rework it to cover for the fact that the ship should be used instead of the boat. Take a look at the CallShip common event to be associated with the Magic Ship and compare it with the CallCanoe common event we created for the Magic Oar back in Chapter 6.

```
@>Control Variables: [0014:MapID] = Map ID
@>Control Variables: [0019:X] = Player's Map X
@>Control Variables: [0020:Y] = Player's Map Y
@>Conditional Branch: Player is Facing Down
  @>Control Variables: [0020:Y] += 1
  @>
: Branch End
@>Conditional Branch: Player is Facing Left
  @>Control Variables: [0020:X] -= 1
  @>
: Branch End
@>Conditional Branch: Player is Facing Right
  @>Control Variables: [0019:X] += 1
  @>
: Branch End
@>Conditional Branch: Player is Facing Up
  @>Control Variables: [0020:Y] -= 1
  @>
: Branch End
@>Get Location Info: [0013], Terrain Tag, Variable [0019][0020]
@>Conditional Branch: Variable [0013:TerrainTag] == 0
  @>Text: -, -, Normal, Bottom
  :     : You can only place the ship in a body of water!
  @>
```

```
: Branch End
@>Conditional Branch: Variable [0013:TerrainTag] == 1
  @>Text: -, -, Normal, Bottom
  :     : You summon the ship!
  @>Set Vehicle Location: Ship, Variable [0014][0019][0020]
  @>
: Branch End
@>Conditional Branch: Variable [0013:TerrainTag] == 2
  @>Text: -, -, Normal, Bottom
  :     : You summon the ship!
  @>Set Vehicle Location: Ship, Variable [0014][0019][0020]
  @>
: Branch End
@>
```

The CallShip event is fairly similar to the CallCanoe event, with the main difference that we define the latter half of the event such that the error message is triggered if the Terrain Tag is equal to 0 and allows the player to summon the ship on both shallow and deep water. Also, you'll want to set the location of the Ship vehicle rather than the Boat vehicle. Last, but perhaps most important, you'll have to set the Deep Water tile Terrain Tag in the Dungeon tileset to 2 (the Deep Water tile is conveniently to the right of the Water tile we set to 1 in Chapter 6).

Hidden Pixies

As noted previously, there are two hidden dwellings within the dungeon level. Both of them contain a single Pixie that will give the player some information when spoken to. For this particular instance, I decided to use a single map to cover both of the dwellings. See Figure 8-3.

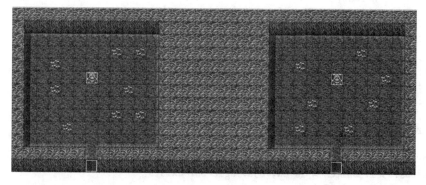

Figure 8-3. The pair of hidden dwellings that the player can find in Pixies' Forest (East). Note the dividing grass wall

You can use large pieces of dividing terrain to stop players from noticing that the map contains areas that are not directly connected. The player can see eight spaces to his/her left and right and about six spaces north and south. As long as you make the terrain bigger than that, the player won't be able to see the difference.

Neat trick, isn't it? The dwelling to the left connects to the first wall of vines near the exit to Pixies' Forest (West) located at 022,002. The dwelling to the right connects to the other marked wall of vines near Lamia (018,027). So, what will the Pixies say? The left Pixie should talk about the player's Magic Oar and how he/she can upgrade it by finding the Pixie on the lone island to the east. Once the player has the Magic Sail, the Pixie should tell the player to find the other hidden dwelling. The second Pixie should talk about Lamia and offer the player a place to rest before he/she heads off to the boss battle. As for the text events themselves, the first Pixie will have a total of four pages, to cover the following:

1. Talking to the player about the Magic Sail

2. Urging the player to get the Magic Sail if he/she hasn't gotten it yet

3. What the Pixie will say once the player has the Magic Sail

4. A final page that covers words the Pixie says once Lamia has been defeated

Page 1 of 4
Condition: 038:Magic Oar exists
@>Text: -, -, Normal, Bottom
:   : Hello!
@>Text: -, -, Normal, Bottom
:   : I sense the presence of a \C[2]Magic Oar\C[0]. My friend
:   : could turn it into a \C[2]Magic Sail\C[0] that will allow
:   : you to summon a greater vessel. You'll need it to
:   : cross the deep water.
@>Text: -, -, Normal, Bottom
:   : You can find her by using the portal hidden behind
:   : the wall of vines to the southwest of my home. Be
:   : careful with the Orcs and the Sahagins!
@>Control Self Switch: A =ON
@>

Page 2 of 4
Conditions: Self Switch A is ON, 038:Magic Oar exists
@>Text: -, -, Normal, Bottom
:   : Hello again! Go get the Magic Sail!
@>

Page 3 of 4
Condition: 039:Magic Sail exists
@>Text: -, -, Normal, Bottom
:   : You have the \C[2]Magic Sail\C[0]! Now, you must make your way
:   : into the deepest part of the forest and destroy
:   : Lamia once and for all.
@>
Page 4 of 4
Condition: Switch 0016:LamiaDefeated is ON, 039:Magic Sail exists
@>Text: -, -, Normal, Bottom
:   : Thank you for all that you have done! Stay safe!
@>

The second Pixie will have two event pages. The first page will be active until the player defeats Lamia. The second page becomes active when the player defeats Lamia.

Page 1 of 2
@>Text: -, -, Normal, Bottom
:   : Lamia's prison is atop the Ancient Temple. Follow
:   : the path to the west of my home.
@>Text: -, -, Normal, Bottom
:   : Would you like to rest?
@>Show Choices: Yes, No
: When [Yes]
  @>Text: -, -, Normal, Bottom
  :   : Sleep well!
  @>Fadeout Screen
  @>Play ME, 'Inn', 100, 100
  @>Wait: 300 frame(s)
  @>Recover All: Entire Party
  @>Fadein Screen
  @>Text: -, -, Normal, Bottom
  :   : Be careful.
  @>
: When [No]
  @>Text: -, -, Normal, Bottom
  :   : Be careful.
  @>
: Branch End
@>
Page 2 of 2
Condition: Switch 0016:LamiaDefeated is ON
@>Text: -, -, Normal, Bottom
:   : May your journeys be filled with light!
@>

The Treasure of Pixies' Forest (East)

This dungeon level has a whopping 11 treasure chests to be opened by the player. As usual, they will be divided into the three distinct types of treasure that we have touched upon during the course of this book. Here are their contents:

1. Character-specific treasure (Palnor/Gust/Feylia)

    - Mythril Sword/Mythril Bow/Mythril Tunic

    - Mythril Chestplate/Mythril Helm/Scroll of Thunder Storm

2. Random treasure

    - Restoration Potion (80%)/Gold Bars (20%)

    - Return Crystal (90%)/Gold Bars (10%)

3. Normal treasure

    - Return Crystal

    - Anti-Crush

    - Restoration Potion

    - Gold Bars

    - Panacea × 2

    - Healing Potion × 2

    - Eye Drops

The game is rapidly approaching its conclusion, so the random chests have a chance to give the player Gold Bars. The extra gold, should the player be so lucky, will be useful for filling any equipment gaps that may remain at this point of the game. Notably, one of the normal chests contains an Anti-Crush, which will halve the damage of Lamia's normal attacks and Trips.

Lamia, the Snake Monster—the Second Boss

Lamia will be our game's second and last boss. As such, this boss event will be rather more nuanced. As the player approaches Lamia, he/she will trigger a pair of text events noting Lamia's presence. Each of the two events will have two pages. See Figure 8-4 for a screenshot of the location of both events.

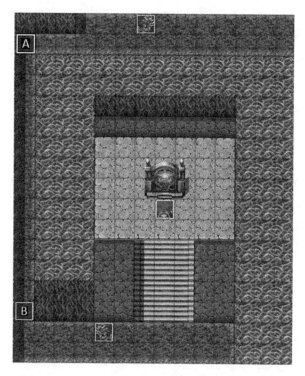

Figure 8-4. *The area surrounding Lamia. Note how Lamia's graphic in the center appears cut off in the map editor. This has no effect on how she appears in the game itself*

Event A
Page 1 of 2
Priority: Below Characters
Trigger: Player Touch
```
@>Text: -, -, Normal, Bottom
:     : You feel a presence wrap around you and shudder
:     : involuntarily.
@>Conditional Branch: Switch [0005:Wrendale] == ON
  @>Text: 'Actor1', 0, Normal, Bottom
  :     : What manner of sorcery is this?
  @>
: Branch End
@>Conditional Branch: Switch [0006:Anabeth] == ON
  @>Text: 'Actor3', 5, Normal, Bottom
  :     : Such horrible energy. Is this Lamia's
  :     : power?
  @>
: Branch End
@>Control Self Switch: A =ON
@>
```

Page 2 of 2
Condition: Self Switch A is ON
Priority: Below Characters
Trigger: Action Button
No Contents

Event B
Page 1 of 2
Priority: Below Characters
Trigger: Player Touch
@>Text: -, -, Normal, Bottom
:   : Harsh whispers find your ear.
@>Text: -, -, Normal, Bottom
:   : Join my cause and free me from my prison!
@>Conditional Branch: Switch [0005:Wrendale] == ON
  @>Text: 'Actor1', 0, Normal, Bottom
  :   : Pay no heed to that monster's words!
  @>
: Branch End
@>Conditional Branch: Switch [0006:Anabeth] == ON
  @>Text: 'Actor3', 5, Normal, Bottom
  :   : We must reach Lamia. Her blight must be
  :   : destroyed at the source!
  @>
: Branch End
@>Control Self Switch: A =ON
@>
Page 2 of 2
Condition: Self Switch A is ON
Priority: Below Characters
Trigger: Action Button
No Contents

As you can see, I decided to give the player's possible companions a little exposure. While the strong and silent companion is more than usable as a game mechanic (especially in such a simple type of game as the one we're making), there's nothing wrong with giving the companions a little personality as well. I use self-switches to make sure that the event only triggers once; otherwise, the player will be trapped in an endless loop when he/she steps on one event or the other.

The boss event itself is two pages long and uses the graphic shown in Figure 8-5 (located in the !BigMonster1 graphic set).

Figure 8-5. *The stock RMVXA graphic for Lamia*

Page 1 of 2
Graphic: See Figure 8-5.
Options: Toggle Stepping Anim. and Direction Fix
Priority: Same as Characters
Trigger: Action Button
Contents
@>Text: -, -, Normal, Bottom
:   : It has been such a long time since I have been free.
:   : That accursed Titania has me sealed away and won't
:   : let me go. You believe me, don't you?
@>Show Balloon Icon: This event, Silence, Wait
@>Text: -, -, Normal, Bottom
:   : No, you don't. Your eyes tell the truth of your
:   : thoughts.
@>Text: -, -, Normal, Bottom
:   : Well then, in that case, there is nothing more to
:   : say.
@>Text: -, -, Normal, Bottom
:   : Lamia attacks!
@>Change Battle BGM: 'Battle7', 100, 100
@>Battle Processing: Lamia
@>

Page 2 of 2
Condition: Switch 0016:LamiaDefeated is ON
Priority: Below Characters
Trigger: Action Button
No Graphic, No Contents

As you can see (and as I promised in Chapter 6 that I would cover), I have the game change the Battle BGM before Lamia attacks the player. This will change the music into something a little more appropriate for a boss battle. Lamia's troop event has four pages. The first one triggers at the start of the battle; the next three trigger at 25% HP intervals.

So, page 2 would trigger when Lamia is at 75% HP remaining, page 3 triggers when she's at half health, and page 4 triggers when she is at 25% HP. Each of the four troop event pages has a Span of Battle (which causes them to trigger only once when their conditions are met).

Page 1 of 4
Condition: Turn No. 0
@>Control Switches: [0016:LamiaDefeated] = ON
@>Text: -, -, Normal, Bottom
:   : I have existed ever since the beginning of time.
:   : I have seen entire nations rise and fall. I will
:   : break out of this prison and assume my rightful
:   : place as the ruler of this world!
@>
Page 2 of 4
Condition: Enemy [1. Lamia]'s HP 75% or below
@>Text: -, -, Normal, Bottom
:   : You are rather pesky, for a human. No matter, that
:   : will make my final victory all the more sweeter.
@>
Page 3 of 4
Condition: Enemy [1. Lamia]'s HP 50% or below
@>Text: -, -, Normal, Bottom
:   : To think that I would be pressed this hard!
@>Text: -, -, Normal, Bottom
:   : Lamia utters words of magic.
@>Force Action: [1.Lamia], [Blizzard], Random
@>Text: -, -, Normal, Bottom
:   : Even in my weakened state, I still have my magic!
@>
Page 4 of 4
Condition: Enemy [1. Lamia]'s HP 25% or below
@>Text: -, -, Normal, Bottom
:   : What are you?!
@>Force Action: [1.Lamia], [Rage], Random
@>

As you can see, I decided to add some banter to Lamia's boss fight. Since the player cannot escape the battle, I flip the LamiaDefeated switch on page 1, which will cause the boss event graphic to disappear from the dungeon level map once the player has defeated Lamia. Note the use of the Force Action command, especially the first instance it is used. Lamia using Blizzard tells the player that she can also cast spells (*only* Blizzard, but it's still a valid warning).

Life After Lamia

So, the player has fought long and hard to defeat the vile snake monster, Lamia. What comes next? The first thing to do is add an Autorun event to the Pixies' Forest (East) map that requires that LamiaDefeated be set to on. It will be two pages long. The most important thing to do in the first page of the event is make sure to change the Battle BGM back to its system default, or the boss BGM will play in every battle.

Page 1 of 2
Priority: Below Characters
Trigger: Autorun
@>Change Battle BGM: 'Battle1', 100, 100
@>Text: -, -, Normal, Bottom
:   : A voice pierces the eerie silence of the deep
:   : forest.
@>Text: -, -, Normal, Bottom
:   : You have done well. Close your eyes.
@>Fadeout Screen
@>Control Self Switch: A =ON
@>Transfer Player:[012:Interior] (012,013), Up
@>
Page 2 of 2
Condition: Self Switch A is ON
Priority: Below Characters
Trigger: Action Button
No Contents

When the player defeats Lamia, Titania teleports the player back to the Pixies' Vale (the exact transfer location puts the player in front of Titania). As you may have inferred, we'll need an Autorun event in the Vale's interior; otherwise, the game will hang with a black screen, as there is no Fadein Screen command to complement the previous Fadeout Screen used. The Vale interior Autorun event is also composed of two pages.

Page 1 of 2
Condition: Switch 0016:LamiaDefeated is ON
Priority: Below Characters
Trigger: Autorun
@>Fadein Screen
@>Text: -, -, Normal, Bottom
:   : You find yourself facing Titania once again.
@>Text: -, -, Normal, Bottom
:   : You have exceeded my expectations, human. You will
:   : forever be welcome here in the Vale. I would reward
:   : you.
@>Text: -, -, Normal, Bottom
:   : You feel a rush of power course through your body.

```
@>Text: -, -, Normal, Bottom
:       : You have gained 1000 EXP!
@>Change EXP: Entire Party, + 1000
@>Text: -, -, Normal, Bottom
:       : You seek the ancient artifact, do you not? It is
:       : buried deep under the forest, under thousands of
:       : years of vegetation. I can send you there with my
:       : magic. You have but to ask.
@>Text: -, -, Normal, Bottom
:       : For now, however, I would like to host a celebration
:       : in your honor.
@>Fadeout Screen
@>Text: -, -, Normal, Bottom
:       : There is much merriment and fun to be had for
:       : several hours.
@>Recover All: Entire Party
@>Text: -, -, Normal, Bottom
:       : Titania calls you back into the Vale's interior
:       : after the festivities.
@>Fadein Screen
@>Text: -, -, Normal, Bottom
:       : I suppose you will want to venture into the Ancient
:       : Temple now.
@>Text: -, -, Normal, Bottom
:       : However, it is important to note that I cannot get
:       : you out of there until you have claimed the artifact.
:       : Make sure you have some way of getting out if you
:       : need a reprieve.
@>Text: -, -, Normal, Bottom
:       : Talk to me again whenever you wish to depart.
@>Control Switches: [0017:AncientTemple] = ON
@>
```

Page 2 of 2
Condition: Switch 0017:AncientTemple is ON
Priority: Below Characters
Trigger: Action Button
No Contents

So, the stage has been set for our game's final level: the player has defeated Lamia and restored peace to the Pixies' Vale. Now, Titania will send the player into the very place that contains the hidden artifact. With that said, here's the final page of Titania's event that I promised earlier to discuss in this chapter.

Page 3 of 3
Condition: Switch 0017: AncientTemple is ON
Graphic: As per previous pages of Titania's event
Priority: Same as Characters
Trigger: Action Button

```
@>Text: -, -, Normal, Bottom
:      : Would you like to go to the Ancient Temple now?
@>Show Choices: Yes, No
: When [Yes]
  @>Conditional Branch: Self Switch B == OFF
    @>Control Variables: [0001:DeepestDungeonFloor] = 6
    @>Control Self Switch: B =ON
    @>Transfer Player:[014:Level 6] (029,043), Up
    @>
  : Else
    @>Transfer Player:[014:Level 6] (029,043), Up
    @>
  : Branch End
  @>
: When [No]
  @>Text: -, -, Normal, Bottom
  :      : Very well. Make ready and talk to me again once
  :      : you are.
  @>
: Branch End
@>
```

There really isn't much to it, save for the fact that it would've broken the flow of the game to cover it in the previous chapter. (You *have* remembered to increase the value of DeepestDungeonFloor throughout the game, haven't you?) The transfer event, logically, is currently useless, but that will change when I cover the Ancient Temple in the next chapter.

Summary

During the course of this chapter, we created the eastern half of the Pixies' Forest, our dungeon crawler's fifth level. The player's Magic Oar was upgraded into a Magic Sail that can summon a ship capable of traveling through deep water. In addition, the player faced down and defeated Lamia, a vicious snake monster being kept in check by Titania. In the next chapter, the player will make his/her way to the Ancient Temple, a timeless locale containing the coveted hidden artifact.

CHAPTER 9

■ ■ ■

The Ancient Temple

In this chapter, we will be working on our dungeon's final level, the Ancient Temple. The player will have to destroy a pair of braziers that form a wall of fire that shields the prize. Enemies are many and at their strongest, as befits a final level.

The Ancient Temple

The player's expected level heading into the Ancient Temple is 15. The game's final level will provide sufficient experience to reach Level 19. Should the player wish to reach the maximum of 20, he/she will have to leave the Temple and return, to prompt the enemies to re-spawn. Here are the things to cover in this chapter.

- **Highly variable encounters**: There will be four new enemy types in this level, the last of which will serve in the capacity of a pair of mini-bosses. When the player collides with an enemy sprite, he/she will be attacked by one of *seven* different troops.

- **The final objective**: The hidden artifact is located at the very back of the Ancient Temple, behind a wall of fire sustained by a pair of braziers. The player must destroy the braziers to reach the artifact.

- **The credits**: Once the player grabs the artifact, the game will end. We will have to provide an event to cover this.

What Does the Town Greeter Have to Say?

To think that we built our city atop the ruins of an ancient temple. Perhaps that is the way of the world: to be built, to decay, and to be built upon again. Be careful with those lost souls that wander the temple...

The town greeter doesn't know too much about the dungeon below; why do you ask?

Level Overview

Our game's final level is a 59×47 sized map with the Dungeon tileset, the Dungeon9 BGM, and a Cobblestones4 and Stone5 battleback. Afterward, see Figure 9-1 for a screenshot of the level in completed form.

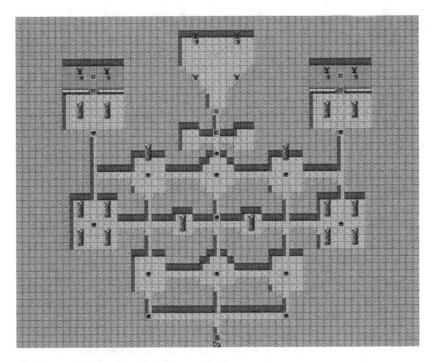

Figure 9-1. *The Ancient Temple*

■ **Note**   The tiles used to create the map are the following: Wall (Stone; the one directly to the left of Wall [Castle]), Cobblestones (located two tiles to the left of Icy Ground), and Wall (Temple).

The first thing about the Ancient Temple that should leap to mind is the total lack of treasure chests. The player has reached the bottom of the dungeon. His/Her only objective is to find the hidden artifact. Everything else is just an obstacle. The rocks behind the player's starting point will return a message if the player interacts with them. Here's the relevant event:

Priority: Same as Characters
Trigger: Action Button
@>Text: -, -, Normal, Bottom
:   : The way out is blocked by rocks. You'll need to
:   : use an item or magic to leave the Ancient Temple.

As Titania had warned toward the end of the previous chapter, the only way out of the Ancient Temple (besides finding the hidden artifact itself and winning the game) is via the Return Crystals or the Return spell.

The Enemies of the Ancient Temple

The game's final level will have enemies representing all those adventurers lost to the dungeon throughout the ages. The encounter event (and battle sprites for each of the enemies) will be covered later in the section. For now, take a look at Table 9-1, to see the stats of each of the four enemies present within the Ancient Temple.

Table 9-1. *List of the Enemies the Player Will Face in the Ancient Temple*

Name	MHP	MMP	ATK	DEF	MAT	MDF	AGI	LUK	HIT %	EVA %	Attack Element
Lost Archer	60	0	22	11	1	5	10	10	100	5	Pierce
Lost Cleric	50	100	18	9	12	12	7	7	100	5	Pierce
Lost Warrior	70	0	25	16	1	1	7	7	100	5	Slash
Dark Priest	200	250	25	15	15	5	5	5	80	0	Crush

The Dark Priest serves as the level's mini-boss. When the player seeks to destroy one of the two braziers blocking entry to the artifact chamber, he/she will have to fight a Dark Priest to gain access to the brazier itself. See Table 9-2 for additional details concerning enemies.

Table 9-2. Item Drops and Skills for the Enemies in the Ancient Temple

Name	EXP	G	Item Drop Slot 1 (Drop Chance)	Item Drop Slot 2 (Drop Chance)	Item Drop Slot 3 (Drop Chance)	Skill List (Rating; Comments)
Lost Archer	100	120	Mythril Bow (1/10)	Mythril Arrow (1/10)	Mythril Chestplate (1/10)	Attack (5), Pierce Shot (5), Triple Shot (8; first used on turn 3 and then used every third turn after that)
Lost Cleric	100	120	Crystal Staff (1/10)	Phoenix Tears (1/5)	Mythril Tunic (1/10)	Attack (5), Heal (8; first used on turn 3 and then used every third turn after that), Sleep (5), Blaze (5)
Lost Warrior	100	120	Mythril Axe (1/10)	Mythril Dagger (1/10)	Adamantine Full Plate (1/10)	Attack (5), Cleave (5), Sand Toss (4)
Dark Priest	250	0	Gold Bars (1/1)	None	None	Attack (1), Umbral Embrace (4; first used on turn 3 and then used on turns 6 and 9), Heal (1; added to action patterns while HP is 50% or less), Umbral Embrace (10; first used on turn 10 and then used every turn until the end of battle), Poison Cloud (1)

The Dark Priest's skill list may appear to be confusing, but it's actually fairly clear-cut. Here's a breakdown of how the first ten turns of combat would look like against the Dark Priest:

1. Attack or Poison Cloud

2. Attack or Poison Cloud

3. Umbral Embrace

4. Attack or Poison Cloud

5. Attack or Poison Cloud

6. Umbral Embrace

7. Attack or Poison Cloud

8. Attack or Poison Cloud

9. Umbral Embrace

10. Umbral Embrace (until the battle ends)

Naturally, Heal gets added to Attack/Poison Cloud turns as a possibility, if the Dark Priest happens to be at 50% HP or less. Really, the battle against the Dark Priest is a race to win before he starts using his strongest attack at every turn. See Table 9-3 for a list of skills created for the enemies of this chapter.

Table 9-3. *List of New Skills Created for the Enemies of the Ancient Temple*

Skill Name	Element	Description	Damage Formula	Notes
Pierce Shot	Pierce	An arrow that pierces its target's armor	a.atk	Used by Lost Archers
Triple Shot	Pierce	Three arrows shoot at random targets	a.atk > b.def ? a.atk - b.def : 1	Used by Lost Archers. Effect achieved via the 3 Random Enemies Scope
Umbral Embrace	None	A malefic attack that does more damage the longer the battle has drawn on	a.mat + $game_variables[6]*5 > b.mdf ? (a.mat + $game_variables[6]*5)- b.mdf : 1	Used by Dark Priests. $game_variables[6] is the variable used to hold the battle's turn count.
Sand Toss	None	Tosses sand at all enemies to attempt to cause Blindness	None	Used by Lost Warriors. Has a 55% chance to cause Blindness

These are the last four skills to be added to the game. Of particular note are Triple Shot's scope (which is three random enemies) and Umbral Embrace, which uses a variable in its damage formula.

■ **Note** The box for damage formulas has all of the functionality of a typical Script event command box. In the case of Umbral Embrace's damage formula, I am using a variable that will cover the battle's turn count.

The Dark Priests

The Ancient Temple houses a pair of Dark Priests, each guarding a brazier blocking access to the ancient artifact. Much like the Living Statues back in Chapter 5, the Dark Priests will disappear from the game permanently when defeated. The event used for the level's mini-bosses is actually simpler than the one we will use for our regular encounters. Each Dark Priest event is two pages long and consists of the following event code. See Figure 9-2 for the Dark Priest's graphic.

Figure 9-2. *Sprite used to represent the Dark Priest on the map. This sprite can be found in the Evil graphic set*

Page 1 of 2
Graphic: See Figure 9-2.
Priority: Same as Characters
Trigger: Action Button
Contents
```
@>Text: -, -, Normal, Bottom
:      : You cannot have the artifact!
@>Battle Processing: Dark Priest
@>Control Self Switch: A =ON
@>
```

The second event page is a standard blank page much like those we have used several times throughout the course of this book. Now, keep in mind that the Dark Priest has a skill that uses a variable to determine its total damage. We want Umbral Embrace to inflict more damage the longer the battle has been in progress. How can we do this? It's really simple. Here's the single troop event page for the Dark Priest:

Condition: When the end of the turn
Span: Turn
@>Control Variables: [0006:turncount] += 1
@>

Yes, seriously. That's all you need. At the end of each turn, the value of turncount will be increased by 1. Of course, the player must battle *two* Dark Priests in this level. If we store the value of turncount and don't erase it at some point, the player will be powerless to beat the second Dark Priest (as the Umbral Embrace will inflict a disproportionately high amount of damage, based on the duration of the first Dark Priest fight). To fix that, you need only have another troop event page (for the sake of consistency, this should be page 1; the preceding code above this paragraph should be page 2).

Condition: Turn No. 0
Span: Battle
@>Control Variables: [0006:turncount] = 0
@>

There you have it! When the player attacks the second Dark Priest, the preceding code will reset the turncount variable, and then the other code will trigger at the end of each turn, counting up appropriately.

The Lost Adventurers

As hinted by the town greeter, lost souls wander the temple's halls. These are the adventurers who have quested for the hidden artifact since the world learned of its existence. They are now bound to protect the artifact until defeated once again. In the spirit of the final level, they are meant more to be a hindrance than actual enemies that the player should try to actively fight. However, should the player decide to do so, the enemies have a chance of dropping the rarest weapons and armor in the game. The event is rather long, despite only having a single page. That is due to the fact that we have seven distinct possibilities for enemy encounters. It's also important to note that the player will be unable to escape any battle in the Ancient Temple. This provides additional incentive to reach the artifact as soon as possible. Figure 9-3 shows the graphic for regular encounters in the Ancient Temple.

Figure 9-3. The sprite graphic used for the regular encounters in the Ancient Temple. You can find this sprite in the Evil graphic set

Graphic: See Figure 9-3
Autonomous Movement: Set Type to Approach, Set Speed to 4: Normal
Priority: Same as Characters
Trigger: Event Touch
Contents
```
@>Control Variables: [0004:d3] = Random No. (1...10)
@>Conditional Branch: Variable [0004:d3] <= 2
  @>Battle Processing: Lost Archer
  @>
: Branch End
@>Conditional Branch: Variable [0004:d3] >= 3
  @>Conditional Branch: Variable [0004:d3] <= 4
    @>Battle Processing: Lost Cleric
    @>
  : Branch End
  @>
: Branch End
@>Conditional Branch: Variable [0004:d3] >= 5
  @>Conditional Branch: Variable [0004:d3] <= 6
    @>Battle Processing: Lost Warrior
    @>
  : Branch End
  @>
: Branch End
@>Conditional Branch: Variable [0004:d3] == 7
  @>Battle Processing: Lost Archer, Lost Cleric
  @>
@>Conditional Branch: Variable [0004:d3] == 8
  @>Battle Processing: Lost Cleric, Lost Warrior
  @>
@>Conditional Branch: Variable [0004:d3] == 9
  @>Battle Processing: Lost Archer, Lost Warrior
  @>
@>Conditional Branch: Variable [0004:d3] == 10
  @>Battle Processing: Lost Archer, Lost Cleric, Lost Warrior
  @>
: Branch End
@>Erase Event
@>
```

Of course, that leaves a single question: What do the enemy battlers look like? During the course of this book, I have only pointed out those battler graphics that are not named as the enemies themselves (the Living Statue, for example). See Figure 9-4 for a look at the battler graphics used for the enemies of the Ancient Temple.

Figure 9-4. *From left to right: Delf_m, Cleric_f, Warrior_m, and Priest. These are used for the Lost Archer, Lost Cleric, Lost Warrior, and Dark Priest enemies, respectively*

Barrier to the End

Only a single wall of fire stands in the way of the player attaining the ancient artifact. Once the player defeats a Dark Priest, he/she will be able to interact with the brazier atop the pedestal and destroy it. Upon destroying both braziers, the area will shake, and the wall of fire will be extinguished. Once the player interacts with the hidden artifact, the game will end. With all of that said, let's take it one step at a time.

The Braziers

Here is the event code for the two braziers that the player must destroy. As is typical of events that have *before* and *after* states, this one will have two pages. Take a look at Figure 9-5 for the red flame brazier graphic.

Figure 9-5. *The red flame brazier graphic used for this event. You can find this graphic in the !Other2 graphic set*

Page 1 of 2
Graphic: See Figure 9-5
Options: Toggle Direction Fix
Priority: Same as Characters
Trigger: Action Button
@>Text: -, -, Normal, Bottom
:   : You see a brazier lit in front of you. Will you
:   : destroy the brazier?
@>Show Choices: Yes, No
: When [Yes]
  @>Text: -, -, Normal, Bottom
  :   : You kick aside the brazier.
  @>Fadeout Screen
  @>Text: -, -, Normal, Bottom
  :   : It crashes to the ground and turns into ash almost
  :   : instantly.
  @>Text: -, -, Normal, Bottom
  :   : You are filled with arcane power!
  @>Change EXP: Entire Party, + 1000
  @>Text: -, -, Normal, Bottom
  :   : You have gained 1000 EXP!
  @>Control Variables: [0007:BraziersDestroyed] += 1
  @>Control Self Switch: A =ON
  @>Fadein Screen
  @>
: When [No]
  @>
: Branch End
@>

Because destroying the braziers is critical to the main quest, I grant the player 1000 experience points for each brazier destroyed. See Figure 9-6 for the smoke graphic.

Figure 9-6. *The smoke graphic used for this event. You can find this graphic in the !Other2 graphic set*

Page 2 of 2
Condition: Self Switch A is ON
Graphic: See Figure 9-6
Options: Toggle Direction Fix
Priority: Same as Characters
Trigger: Action Button
@>Text: -, -, Normal, Bottom
:   : You see a cloud of ash on the ground.
@>

The Wall of Fire

The barrier preventing the player from reaching the hidden artifact is a four-tile-long path of fire. Each individual square is its own event, but they will all be the same. The wall of fire events are located at (029,013), (029,014), (029,015), and (029,016) See Figure 9-7 for the relevant fire graphic and then look below that to see the event code.

Figure 9-7. The fire graphic used for this event. You can find it in the !Other2 graphic set

Page 1 of 2
Graphic: See Figure 9-7
Options: Toggle Direction Fix
Priority: Same as Characters
Trigger: Action Button
@>Text: -, -, Normal, Bottom
:   : The wall of fire blocks the path!
@>

Page 2 of 2
Condition: Variable 0007:BraziersDestroyed is 2 or above
Priority: Below Characters
Trigger: Action Button
No Graphic, No Contents

All four squares of the fire wall poof out of existence the moment the player destroys the second brazier. Because giving the player feedback is always a good thing, let's add an Autorun event that triggers when the player destroys the second brazier, telling him/her that the wall of fire has been extinguished.

Page 1 of 2
Condition: Variable 0007:BraziersDestroyed is 2 or above
Priority: Below Characters
Trigger: Autorun
Contents
```
@>Wait: 60 frame(s)
@>Shake Screen: 5, 5, @60
@>Flash Screen: (255,255,255,255), @60, Wait
@>Wait: 30 frame(s)
@>Text: -, -, Normal, Bottom
:     : The wall of fire blocking the artifact collapses!
@>Control Self Switch: A =ON
@>
```

Page 2 of 2
Condition: Self Switch A is ON
Priority: Below Characters
Trigger: Action Button
No Contents

The Ancient Artifact

With the braziers destroyed, the player can finally claim what he/she has sought for six dungeon levels. So, what happens once the player interacts with the artifact? He/She wins, of course! First, see Figure 9-8 for the graphic to be used for our artifact event, then scroll past that to see the event code.

Figure 9-8. The green orb graphic used for the artifact event. You can find it in !Other1

Priority: Same as Characters
Trigger: Action Button
@>Text: -, -, Normal, Bottom
:   : You see a pale green orb. Will you take it?
@>Show Choices: Yes, No
: When [Yes]
  @>Text: -, -, Normal, Bottom
  :   : You hear Titania's voice in your head.
  @>Text: -, -, Normal, Bottom
  :   : I sense that you have attained the artifact. Allow
  :   : me to transport you back to the Vale.
  @>Fadeout Screen
  @>Fadeout BGM: 3 sec.
  @>Conditional Branch: Switch [0001:Palnor] == ON
    @>Text: -, -, Normal, Bottom
    :   : After reaching the Vale, Palnor made his way out of
    :   : the dungeon and left Eagle's Crossing for the
    :   : highlands.
    @>Text: -, -, Normal, Bottom
    :   : The artifact did not work as Palnor had expected.
    :   : It had only the power to revive a single human.
    :   : The lucky recipient of the orb's magic was the
    :   : chieftain's daughter.
    @>Text: -, -, Normal, Bottom
    :   : She decided to accompany Palnor, as he swore to
    :   : continue adventuring until he could see the rest
    :   : of his people returned to life.
    @>
  : Branch End
  @>Conditional Branch: Switch [0002:Gust] == ON
    @>Text: -, -, Normal, Bottom
    :   : After reaching the Vale, Gust spent a few days
    :   : celebrating with the Pixies. He then made his way to
    :   : Eagle's Crossing and out into the desert.
    @>Text: -, -, Normal, Bottom
    :   : To his own horror, Gust realized that his love had
    :   : been removed from her tomb. With tempered resolve,
    :   : Gust stoically walked into the desert city of Lazul.
    :   : Someone had to know what had happened to her...
    @>
  : Branch End
  @>Conditional Branch: Switch [0003:Feylia] == ON
    @>Text: -, -, Normal, Bottom
    :   : After reaching the Vale, Feylia took some time to
    :   : analyze the strange artifact she had risked her life
    :   : for. She realized that the magic contained within
    :   : was unlike anything anyone had ever harnessed.

```
    @>Text: -, -, Normal, Bottom
      :      : Satisfied of her find, she struck out to the western
      :      : lands. With the power of her magic, she willed her
      :      : sibling back to life.
    @>Text: -, -, Normal, Bottom
      :      : However, a nagging thought remained in Feylia's
      :      : mind. What sort of being created the artifact?
      :      : Would they be any danger to the greater world?
      :      : Her brother at her side, Feylia made her way
    @>Text: -, -, Normal, Bottom
      :      : back to her magic school. She had to learn more...
    @>
    : Branch End
  @>
: When [No]
  @>
: Branch End
@>Wait: 120 frame(s)
@>Play BGM: 'Theme1', 100, 100
@>Text(S): Speed 2
  :       : CREDITS:
  :       :
  :       : Me - For making this game.
  :       :
  :       : You - For playing it.
  :       :
  :       : Enterbrain - For making RPG Maker VX Ace.
  :       : Without it, this game would not exist.
  :       :
  :       : THANKS FOR PLAYING!
@>Return to Title Screen
@>
```

Pretty beefy event, isn't it? Yet, there's not much to it. In a nutshell

- The player interacts with the artifact.

- The game asks the player if he/she wishes to grab the artifact.

- If no, nothing happens.

- If yes, the screen fades out and a postgame message is written out, depending on the player character.

- Afterward, the credits are played and the game returns the player to the title screen.

Note how each of the ending messages gives a plot hook that can be used to extend the game. Speaking of extending the game, I'm going to tackle an alternate situation before we move on to the final chapter of this book. What if the player has to escape the dungeon without the aid of Return (the spell or the item)?

The Great Escape

After countless trials and tribulations, the player has finally attained the ancient artifact. However, doing so has awoken an equally ancient spirit, and that spirit is *not* pleased. It will chase the player and attack him/her until it has defeated the player, or until the player has stepped onto the staircase leading into Eagle's Crossing. We will use common events to have the enemy attack the player at regular intervals. Once the player reaches Eagle's Crossing, he/she wins the game.

The Ancient Spirit

The first order of business is to create the enemy that will haunt our player as he/she makes his/her way back up the dungeon. The enemy battler sprite to be used is Ghost. See Figure 9-9 for a screenshot of the Ancient Spirit's relevant information.

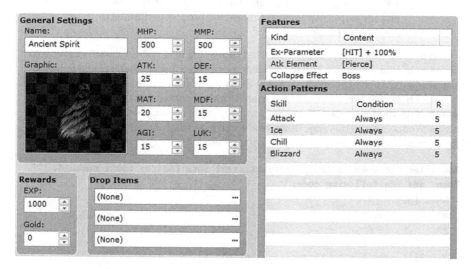

Figure 9-9. The Ancient Spirit. Note that it drops no items or gold when defeated

The Ancient Spirit has twice the health of the Dark Priests that the player defeated to acquire the hidden artifact. In a manner of speaking, it has the power to be a final boss. Yet, how the player will be engaged by this foe is a very unique affair.

Encountering the Ancient Spirit

For the purposes of this exercise, I will be adding a third choice to the yes/no the player is given upon interacting with the ancient artifact. When the player selects the third choice, a common event named StepsToAncientSpirit will be called. After the common event code has run its course, the ArtifactGet switch will be flipped on, and a second common event (AncientSpiritEncounter) with a Parallel Process trigger will be called. This is what this sequence of events will do:

- In StepsToAncientSpirit, we use a pair of variables to hold a static number (StepsN) and the player's current number of steps taken (StepsTaken). Then, we use the Script event command to add two random numbers and one static number together, based on the value of StepsN. We save the result to the StepsToEncounter variable.

- We turn on the ArtifactGet switch and call the AncientSpiritEncounter event.

- AncientSpiritEncounter uses another variable called StepsTakenOnMap to determine how many steps the player has taken toward encountering the Ancient Spirit. A conditional branch checks to see if StepsTakenOnMap is greater than or equal to StepsToEncounter. If it is, the player is attacked by the Ancient Spirit.

- If the player wins the battle, we set StepsToEncounter to 100 and jump back to the start of the common event. If the player escapes the battle, we repeat the process performed in StepsToAncientSpirit.

Why is this necessary? In essence, what I am doing here is using common events to create a random encounter. You're probably considering the fact that it would be easier just to add the Ancient Spirit encounter to every level of our game and then use the Change Encounter event command to enable random encounters once the player has acquired the hidden artifact. That is only true if you have a single enemy you want the player to encounter in this way. Otherwise, you'll have to apply this method. First, have the code that needs to be added to the artifact event.

Add Alternate Path to the already existent Show Choices event command. Then, add the following code:

```
: When [No]
  @>Jump to Label: No
  @>
: When [Alternate Path]
  @>Call Common Event: [StepsToAncientSpirit]
  @>Text: -, -, Normal, Bottom
  :      : You grab the artifact and feel a malevolent presence
  :      : enter the area!
  @>Text: -, -, Normal, Bottom
  :      : You must escape the dungeon! Beware, for the power
  :      : of the Ancient Spirit prevents escape through
  :      : magical means!
  @>Jump to Label: Run!
  @>
: Branch End
```

Below Return To Title Screen, add the following code:

```
@>Label: Run!
@>Transfer Player:[013:Level 5] (014,037), Down
@>Label: No
@>
```

So, when the alternate path is taken, the player will receive a warning message and will be spirited away to Level 5 (the exact destination is where Lamia used to stand before being defeated). From there, the player must make his/her way to the surface. Now, here's the code for both of the common events to be used for this exercise:

StepsToAncientSpirit
```
@>Control Variables: [0010:StepsN] = 20
@>Control Variables: [0008:StepsTaken] = Steps
@>Script: n = $game_variables[10]
  :     : $game_variables[9] = 18 + rand(n) + rand (n)
@>Control Switches: [0018:ArtifactGet] = ON
@>Call Common Event: [AncientSpiritEncounter]
@>
```

■ **Note** Instead of using StepsN to hold the value of n, you could define n within the Script event command. I did it this slightly longer way, as it makes it a bit easier to change the value of n when desired. rand is a Ruby method for creating random numbers. You pass rand a parameter telling it the range of values that you want it to pick from, so, for example, rand (6) will pick randomly from a sequence of six values. Ruby is zero-based, so the sequence begins at 0. rand(6) will provide a random number from 0 to 5. If you want to emulate a die roll and start from 1, just add 1 to the final result. So, rand(6)+1 will give you a result between the range of 1 and 6. So, in the case of the preceding code, the number saved to $game_variables[9] is 18 plus the sum of two random numbers (as picked by the rand method) that range from 0 to 19.

AncientSpiritEncounter
Trigger: Parallel Process
Condition Switch: 0018:ArtifactGet
```
@>Label: Restart
@>Control Variables: [0011:StepsTakenOnMap] = Steps
@>Control Variables: [0011:StepsTakenOnMap] -= Variable [0008:StepsTaken]
@>Conditional Branch: Variable [0011:StepsTakenOnMap] >= Variable
[0009:StepsToEncounter]
  @>Battle Processing: Ancient Spirit
  : If Win
    @>Jump to Label: Bonus
    @>
  : If Escape
    @>Jump to Label: Resolve
    @>
  : Branch End
  @>
```

```
: Branch End
@>Conditional Branch: Switch [0092] == ON
  @>Label: Resolve
  @>Control Variables: [0008:StepsTaken] = Steps
  @>Control Variables: [0010:StepsN] = 20
  @>Script: n = $game_variables[10]
  :          : $game_variables[9] = 18 + rand(n) + rand (n)
  @>Jump to Label: Restart
  @>
: Branch End
@>Conditional Branch: Switch [0092] == ON
  @>Label: Bonus
  @>Control Variables: [0008:StepsTaken] = Steps
  @>Control Variables: [0010:StepsN] = 100
  @>Jump to Label: Restart
  @>
: Branch End
@>
```

■ **Note**   The pair of conditional branches requiring that Switch 92 be onare used to ensure that the code within is executed only if jumped into via an appropriate label.

So, what happens when the player is attacked by the Ancient Spirit? The Ancient Spirit has four troop event pages. I wanted this particular battle to be special, so I made it so that the battle ends on the fourth turn after starting. Any damage the player manages to inflict on the Ancient Spirit will persist between battles. If the player should manage to drop the Ancient Spirit's HP to 0, it will be defeated and allow the player 100 steps of reprieve before attacking again. With that said, here are the four troop event pages for the Ancient Spirit battle.

Page 1 of 4
Condition: Turn No. 0
Span: Battle
```
@>Change Enemy State: Entire Troop, + [Immortal]
@>Change Enemy HP: Entire Troop, - Variable [0021:SpiritDamage]
@>Control Variables: [0012:SpiritCurrentHP] = [1. AncientSpirit]'s HP
@>Control Variables: [0021:SpiritDamage] = 500 - $game_variables[12]
@>
```

Page 2 of 4
Condition: When the end of the turn
Span: Turn
```
@>Control Variables: [0012:SpiritCurrentHP] = [1. Ancient Spirit]'s HP
@>Control Variables: [0021:SpiritDamage] = 500 - $game_variables[12]
@>
```

Page 3 of 4
Condition: Turn No. 4
@>Control Variables: [0008:StepsTaken] = Steps
@>Control Variables: [0010:StepsN] = 20
@>Script: n = $game_variables[10]
:   : $game_variables[9] = 18 + rand(n) + rand (n)
@>Abort Battle
@>

Page 4 of 4
Condition: Enemy [1.Ancient Spirit]'s HP 0% or below
Span: Battle
@>Control Variables: [0012:SpiritCurrentHP] = 500
@>Control Variables: [0021:SpiritDamage] = 0
@>Change Enemy State: Entire Troop, - [Immortal]
@>

At the start of the battle (page 1), we give the Ancient Spirit the Immortal state (the sole purpose of applying this state is so that we can execute page 4 of its troop event if necessary). Then, we lower the enemy's HP by an amount equal to the value of the SpiritDamage variable. Afterward, we save the Ancient Spirit's current HP into the SpiritCurrentHP variable and save the difference between 500 (the Ancient Spirit's maximum HP) and SpiritCurrentHP to the SpiritDamage variable. This is done because each battle with the Ancient Spirit lasts a maximum of four turns, so we want to keep track of its HP between battles (a given battle can end earlier if the Ancient Spirit drops to 0 HP, as coded in page 4 of its troop event).

■ **Tip**   You can use the Script Operand in Control Variables to write equations.

At the end of each turn (page 2), we check the Ancient Spirit's HP and save the appropriate values to SpiritDamage and SpiritCurrentHP. On the fourth turn (page 3), the battle is aborted, but not before setting StepsTaken to the player's current number of steps and using the Script snippet to set the value of StepsToEncounter ($game_variables[9]) to determine when the player will next encounter the Ancient Spirit. The fourth and last page is triggered if the Ancient Spirit's HP is reduced to 0. In that case, we set SpiritCurrentHP to 500 and SpiritDamage to 0 (effectively resetting the enemy's HP in preparation for the next fight) and remove Immortal, so that the Ancient Spirit can be properly defeated.

No Return, Yes Escape

So, as noted immediately before the start of the Great Escape section, the player will be unable to use Return in any shape or form to escape the dungeon. Instead, he/she must break free of the dungeon the long way. To accomplish this, we'll have to edit the relevant Return common events.

■ **Tip**   You can adapt the event code we used back in Chapter 6 to prevent the player from using Return to leave the room Kerberos appeared in.

For the sake of completeness, here's what you should add to the relevant common events.

```
@>Conditional Branch: Switch [0018:ArtifactGet] == ON
  @>Text: -, -, Normal, Bottom
  :      : The power of the Ancient Spirit blocks the use of
  :      : Return!
  @>Jump to Label: Lock
  @>
: Branch End
```

Last, but not least important, we must disable the portal in the Pixies' Vale that leads directly to Eagle's Crossing (as easy as adding a second event page that lacks a transfer event and gives an error message concerning the Ancient Spirit) and edit the transfer event that leads back to Eagle's Crossing on the first dungeon level. The former should be easy enough to add, so I'll leave it to you, as an exercise. Following, you can see the event code for the latter. (This code is an adaptation of preexisting event code for the Parallel Process transfer event on Level 1.)

```
@>Control Variables: [0019:X] = Player's Map X
@>Control Variables: [0020:Y] = Player's Map Y
@>Conditional Branch: Variable [0019:X] == 10
  @>Conditional Branch: Variable [0020:Y] == 23
    @>Conditional Branch: Switch [0018:ArtifactGet] == OFF
      @>Transfer Player:[001:Eagle's Crossing] (012,004), Down
      @>
    : Branch End
    @>
  : Branch End
  @>
: Branch End
@>Conditional Branch: Variable [0019:X] == 10
  @>Conditional Branch: Variable [0020:Y] == 23
    @>Conditional Branch: Switch [0018:ArtifactGet] == ON
      @>Text: -, -, Normal, Bottom
      :      : You have escaped the dungeon with the artifact!
      @>Fadeout Screen
      @>Control Switches: [0018:ArtifactGet] = OFF
      @>Wait: 120 frame(s)
      @>Play BGM: 'Theme1', 100, 100
      @>Text(S): Speed 2
      :         : CREDITS:
```

```
      :               :
      :               : Me - For making this game.
      :               :
      :               : You - For playing it.
      :               :
      :               : Enterbrain - For making RPG Maker VX Ace.
      :               : Without it, this game would not exist.
      :               :
      :               : THANKS FOR PLAYING!
      @>Return to Title Screen
      @>
    : Branch End
    @>
  : Branch End
  @>
: Branch End
@>
```

As you can see, while ArtifactGet is off, the player will be returned to Eagle's Crossing normally. However, stepping on the exit staircase when ArtifactGet is on will result in the player's victory. He/She receives a congratulatory message, the ArtifactGet switch is turned off, and the credits are rolled. At the end of it all, the player will be looking at the title screen once again.

Congratulations!

As per the section title, I do believe that congratulations are in order. You have just completed your very own 2D role-playing game in a single weekend! Give yourself a pat on the back and a round of applause. You deserve it! Now, you are armed with the necessary tools to continue working on this game (or any other game concept you come up with in the future). With that said, there is still one chapter left in this book. It will cover things I did not cover in these first nine chapters. For starters, I'll finally talk about that mysterious nonplayer character in the lower-right corner of Eagle's Crossing. Look forward to it!

Summary

During the course of this chapter, we created the Ancient Temple, our game's final level. The player fought his/her way through the lost souls of the past to defeat a pair of Dark Priests blocking braziers. Those braziers were sustaining a wall of fire that prevented the player from reaching the hidden artifact and winning the game. Upon reaching and grabbing the artifact, the player finds out what happens next with his/her character of choice. An alternate hypothetical situation was explored as well. In this book's final chapter, I will discuss several interesting ways to expand the game that we have created together.

185

■ ■ ■

CHAPTER 10

What Comes Next

This chapter focuses on features we can add to our game to make it more lively and to add complexity. As promised, the first topic concerns the mysterious nonplayer character (NPC) that lives in the southeastern corner of Eagle's Crossing.

The Bazaar NPC

This particular NPC runs a shop unlike any other in our game. Instead of the static list of items every other shop provides, his shop is stocked with random items. It didn't really seem appropriate to discuss him in previous chapters, given the fact that he gave the player nothing that couldn't already be attained in another shop. However, I think the whole concept of a shop with a random inventory is cool, so let's begin.

Overview

Here is a list of things you'll require to create a bazaar:

- The NPC itself

- A script page that contains the logic for the addition of random items to a shop list

- The list of items, armor, and weapons that you would like the bazaar to have on offer

- A common event that uses a pair of conditional branches to ensure that the bazaar list isn't rerolled until desired

Perhaps the most involved part of this NPC is the script page, so let's begin with that.

Shop Processing—Scripting Style

To script the Bazaar, we must first understand how to use scripting to emulate the Shop Processing event command. Go to the Script Editor (by left-clicking the Script Editor option within the Tools submenu at the top of the application; alternatively, pressing F11 will open the Script Editor as well) and run a search for "Shop Processing." You can run searches within the Script Editor by pressing the Ctrl, Shift, and F keys at the same time (alternatively, right-clicking any part of the script list located on the left side of the Script Editor dialog menu will bring up several commands, of which Find happens to be the very last one). RPG Maker VX Ace (RMVXA) will return a single result. Clicking it should send you to the following code (located in Game_Interpreter):

```
def command_302
  return if $game_party.in_battle
  goods = [@params]
  while next_event_code == 605
    @index += 1
    goods.push(@list[@index].parameters)
  end
  SceneManager.call(Scene_Shop)
  SceneManager.scene.prepare(goods, @params[4])
  Fiber.yield
end
```

Starting from the top,

- def is used in Ruby to denote a **method definition**. In this case, the method's name is command_302.

- Recall how events work: they execute from top to bottom, unless you use Labels to skip ahead or backtrack. Code in Ruby works the same way. return serves as an escape clause, in a manner of speaking, that stops executing code when reached. In this case, execution of the command_302 method will prematurely end if the player is in battle (the reason being, as you can imagine, that you can't enter shops while in battle).

- The goods variable contains the list of items that are to be sold at a particular shop. The brackets after the equal sign signify an **array**. Fittingly enough, an array in Ruby is a list of items. @params is an instance variable that fills the array.

- while is a type of loop. The code contained within the loop will be executed as long as the expression to the right of the while remains true. next_event_code is an internal value used for a lot of RMVXA's event commands. All you have to know in this case is that 605 is the value that next_event_code holds when it has not yet completed adding items to the shop.

- Within the loop itself, you can see that the value of @index (another instance variable) is increased by 1 for every time the loop is executed.

- .push is an array method that, as its name implies, adds an item to the end of the current array.

- From there to the end, the rest of the method is fairly clear-cut. Basically, the Shop Scene is called, and then the shop is prepared. As noted, the list of items is contained in the goods parameter. @params[4] determines whether the shop allows or disallows a sale.

Some (or all) of this may seem confusing, but Archeia (over at the official RPG Maker web site) created a thread that covers (among other things) Script calls for Shop Processing. Here's a related link containing the relevant code: http://forums. rpgmakerweb.com/index.php?/topic/25891-script-calls-for-shop-processing/. And, for the sake of convenience, you'll find the code in question following:

```
goods = [[type, id, price_override_flag(, price)]]
SceneManager.call(Scene_Shop)
SceneManager.scene.prepare(goods, true)

# Example Script Call:
goods = [[0,1,1,25],[0,2,0]]
SceneManager.call(Scene_Shop)
SceneManager.scene.prepare(goods, true)

# You can also use a loop to add the elements to the array:
goods = []
for id in 1..20
  goods.push([0, id, 0])
end
```

The preceding code should make things a lot easier to understand. To illustrate, let's take the sample script call and package it into a module within the Script Editor.

- Open the Script Editor and scroll down to the Materials section.

- Once there, right-click (Insert Here) and then click Insert. Doing so will add a blank space above (Insert Here).

- Left-click the blank space, find the Name field in the lower-left corner of the Script Editor interface, and name this script page Shop Example.

- Then, add the following code to that page:

```
module Example
  module_function

  def shop
    goods = [[0,1,1,25],[0,2,0]]
    SceneManager.call(Scene_Shop)
    SceneManager.scene.prepare(goods, true)
  end
end
```

As before, let's take this from the top.

- I created a **module** called Example, to contain the sample code.

- The module_function nested within the module is necessary for the correct functioning of the module. (Alternatively, you could add self to each method definition within the module. In the case of the preceding code, you could have def self.shop).

- I define a **method** called shop to directly handle the scripted shop logic.

- Then, I copy-paste the example code into the shop method.

- Last, I closed both the method and module definitions with appropriate end statements.

With that code added to the Script Editor, all that remains to be done is to use the Script event command to call it from within the game itself. For this purpose, I created a single NPC with a single line of code.

```
Script: Example.shop
```

When the player interacts with that NPC, a shop will come up. According to how the Items tab of my Database has been organized, the preceding code should result in me seeing Lesser Healing Potions on sale for 25 gold and Lesser Magic Potions for 20 gold. How can I be so sure of this? Well, let's take another look at the very first line of code I copy-pasted from the relevant forum thread.

```
goods = [[type, id, price_override_flag(, price)]]
```

This is the format for individual items that get saved into *goods*, and it holds four parameters.

1. type refers to the item type within RMVXA. Items are 0, Weapons are 1, and Armors are 2. So, both of the shop items in the example script call are Items.

2. id refers to the ID number of the item, weapon, or armor within the RMVXA Database. As we created these two potions first (all the way back in Chapter 2, in fact), the sample items should be Lesser Healing Potion and Lesser Magic Potion, respectively.

3. `price_override_flag` is the Script equivalent of the **Price** box in the Shop Processing event command dialog menu. If set to 0 (`false`), the item's price will be set to its default. If set to 1 (`true`), you must define the item's new price.

4. `price` is only needed if you have set `price_override_flag` to 1. In that case, you would set here the new price for the item in question.

Of course, you're probably looking at this and wondering how you can make a random shop. Well, read on, and I'll tell you all about how I did it.

Creating the Bazaar

Because we want to create a shop that has random items, we need a way to randomize what gets plugged into the item arrays for goods. We can use `rand` to much the same effect as we did in the previous chapter. For the sake of simplicity, the price override flag will always be on, so the price of the item will be randomized as well. Here's a breakdown of the bazaar script functionality:

- The method for the shop will accept a single parameter called `value`. Value determines the number of items that the shop will hold.

- The main engine of the shop will be a `while` loop that triggers while `value` is greater than 0.

- Two local variables called `type` and `mod` will randomize the item type and item price modifier, respectively. `type`'s value is calculated via `rand(3)`, while `mod`'s value is calculated via `rand(4)`. After getting the value of `mod`, I then use an equation to get the proper price modifier (`(mod*0.5) + 0.5`). Depending on the value of `rand(4)`, the price modifier will be between half to two times the original item's price.

- I use the `case` method to randomize the item ID, based on its previously determined `type`. `id` is the variable in charge of holding the ID number. At this time, I set the base price of the item (as defined in the Database) and place it in the `price` local variable.

- When `type` is 0, `id` is equal to `1 + rand(14)`. `price` is equal to `$data_items[id].price`.

- When `type` is 1, `id` is equal to `1 + rand(40)`. `price` is equal to `$data_weapons[id].price`.

- When `type` is 2, `id` is equal to `1 + rand(28)`. `price` is equal to `$data_armors[id].price`.

■ **Note** The data of items, weapons, and armor are contained within arrays, one for each individual object of interest. Price is one of those many parameters, hence the reason why you can call to the price of an object, as I am doing here. Price is contained within RPG::Item, one of the many hard-coded classes of RMVXA.

- Once the item's type, price modifier, base price, and ID have been determined, we make it so that price is equal to (price*mod).to_i. .to_i makes sure that the value contained in price is expressed as an integer.

- Then, after *that* is done, we can push the completed item into the goods variable. To conclude, the value of value is reduced by 1.

- If value reaches 0, the script breaks out of the while loop and calls up the shop.

With the preceding information in hand, you are now ready to see the code for this special shop.

```
module Bazaar
  module_function

  def code(value)
    goods = []
        while value > 0
        type = rand(3)
        mod = rand(4)
        mod = (mod*0.5) + 0.5
        case type
        when 0
          id = 1 + rand(14)
          price = $data_items[id].price
        when 1
          id = 1 + rand(40)
          price = $data_weapons[id].price
        else
          id = 1 + rand(22)
          price = $data_armors[id].price
        end
        price = (price*mod).to_i
        goods.push([type, id, 1, price])
        value = value - 1
      end
```

```
    SceneManager.call(Scene_Shop)
    SceneManager.scene.prepare(goods, true)
    $game_variables[3] = goods
  end

  def call
    SceneManager.call(Scene_Shop)
    SceneManager.scene.prepare($game_variables[3], true)
  end
end
```

Finishing Up the Bazaar

With the scripting out of the way, we need only create a common event to keep the bazaar from re-randomizing until desired. It is as easy as the following event code:

```
@>Conditional Branch: Switch [0010:Bazaar] == ON
  @>Script: Bazaar.call
  @>
: Branch End
@>Conditional Branch: Switch [0010:Bazaar] == OFF
  @>Control Switches: [0010:Bazaar] = ON
  @>Script: Bazaar.code(5)
  @>
: Branch End
@>
```

■ **Note**   The "5" in parentheses after `Bazaar.code` is the number that will be assigned to the `value` variable in the script. You can replace that with whichever number tickles your fancy, to have as many items as you need in the shop.

Finally, whichever NPC you decide to assign as your bazaar shopkeeper requires only the following line of code:

```
@>Call Common Event: [Bazaar]
```

Figure 10-1 shows a sample roll of the Bazaar.

193

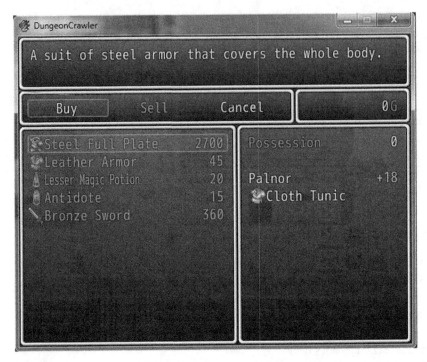

Figure 10-1. A five-item Bazaar. Note how some of the items are not at their base price

So, here are some things to consider when using this code:

- There is a possibility that you will receive two copies of the same item, given that the script has no way of checking against that.

■ **Note** You can add anti-duplication checks to the Bazaar shop once you gain some more scripting knowledge. All you would have to do is check to see if the item already exists in the new array and re-roll if it does.

- If you want the shop's inventory to change, you'll have to turn off the Bazaar switch. Some good times to allow the shop to re-roll its stock include when the player reaches a new level, the player rests at an inn, or when an important plot point is reached.

- You can tweak mod so that the prices vary a little more. Just make sure that you don't create a situation in which it is cheaper to buy an item than to sell it. (The default selling price is half of the purchase price.) Should that occur, the player will have a trivial way to receive infinite gold.

The Next Leg of the Journey

The player has acquired the hidden artifact and seen the endgame credits. However, the beauty of a dungeon crawler is that there can always be more dungeons to crawl. In this section, I will cover the following:

- Creating a portal event that activates at certain "steps taken" intervals.

- If the player uses the portal, he/she will be taken to one of three special mini-dungeons that lead to a fourth mini-dungeon.

- The final mini-dungeon will have a pair of exits that lead to a treasure room. The player will have to take both exits to get all of the dungeon's treasure.

- Once the player has completed the dungeon, he/she will be returned to Eagle's Crossing.

A Portal Appears

The first order of business is to create a portal that does the following:

- Appears when the player's step count is a multiple of 250

- Stays open until the player has taken 100 steps

- Closes until the next time the player's step count is a multiple of 250

- Sends the player to one of three random locations

To accomplish this, we'll need a Parallel Process event to handle the portal's appearance and subsequent disappearance and an Action Button event for the actual portal. The Parallel Process event will have a total of two pages, and the portal event will have a single page. Here's the first page of the Parallel Process event.

```
@>Control Variables: [0008:StepsTaken] = Steps
@>Control Variables: [0022:PortalCount] = $game_variables[8] % 250
@>Conditional Branch: Variable [0022:PortalCount] == 0
  @>Text: -, -, Normal, Bottom
  :     : A portal has materialized in the area!
  @>Control Variables: [0022:PortalCount] = Variable [0008:StepsTaken]
  @>Control Variables: [0022:PortalCount] += 100
  @>Control Switches: [0020:PortalOpen] = ON
  @>
: Branch End
@>
```

Perhaps the most interesting line of the preceding code is the second one. What's up with that percent symbol? That is the modulus operator, which gives an alternate result for division. Let's say that StepsTaken is equal to 125. 125 divided by 250 would be 0.5. However, the result of 125 % 250 is 125. Why? What the modulus operator is giving you is the remainder left after the nearest whole division. So, for example, 10 mod 3 returns 1, because 3 goes into 10 three times (to give 9), leaving 1. 11 mod 3 would be 2, and 12 mod 3 would be 0, because 12 divides by 3 exactly. It's those exact divisions that we're looking for. Going back to our event code, we get the aforementioned exact divisions at intervals of 250 (250, 500, 750, etc.). This is what we require to ensure the portal is opening at the correct step intervals.

■ **Note** You can find a neat modulus operator calculator at www.miniwebtool.com/modulo-calculator/.

After that realization, the rest of the event should be rather clear. When PortalCount is equal to 0, the player will receive a message notifying him/her that the portal has opened. Then, the value of PortalCount is set to that of StepsTaken and subsequently increased by 100 (that will keep the portal open for 100 steps). Finally, the PortalOpen switch is set to on, which leads to the second page in this Parallel Process event.

```
@>Control Variables: [0008:StepsTaken] = Steps
@>Conditional Branch: Variable [0022:PortalCount] == Variable
[0008:StepsTaken]
  @>Text: -, -, Normal, Bottom
  :     : The portal has closed!
  @>Control Variables: [0022:PortalCount] = Steps
  @>Control Switches: [0020:PortalOpen] = OFF
  @>
: Branch End
@>
```

Because we want to compare the value of StepsTaken with the value of PortalCount, we use Control Variables to keep StepsTaken updated. Once StepsTaken catches up to PortalCount, we display a message declaring that the portal has closed, set the value of PortalCount to the player's Steps count, and then turn off the PortalOpen switch, returning the Parallel Process event to page 1.

Using the Portal

The portal spawning and closing events are nice and all, but we need an event that represents the portal itself. As with most events that require interaction, I'll make this one have a Same as Characters priority with an Action Button trigger.

```
Condition: 0020:PortalOpen is ON
@>Text: -, -, Normal, Bottom
:       : You see a portal before you. Will you step through?
@>Show Choices: Yes, No
: When [Yes]
  @>Text: -, -, Normal, Bottom
  :       : You step through the portal.
  @>Control Variables: [0004:d3] = Random No. (1...3)
  @>Conditional Branch: Variable [0004:d3] == 1
    @>Transfer Player:[026:Bonus Dungeon] (006,006), Down
    @>
  : Branch End
  @>Conditional Branch: Variable [0004:d3] == 2
    @>Transfer Player:[026:Bonus Dungeon] (033,005), Down
    @>
  : Branch End
  @>Conditional Branch: Variable [0004:d3] == 3
    @>Transfer Player:[026:Bonus Dungeon] (009,035), Down
    @>
  : Branch End
  @>
: When [No]
  @>
: Branch End
@>
```

When the player steps through the portal, we store a random number between 1 and 3 in the d3 variable. The player is sent to a mini-dungeon dependent on what number is present in d3 at that time. See Figure 10-2 for a picture of the extra dungeon.

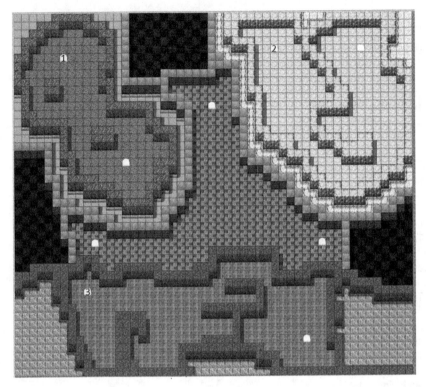

Figure 10-2. *The dungeon to which the portal leads. Note that each of the three individual locations are marked numerically*

If d3 is equal to 1, the player will be sent to the northwestern quadrant. If d3 is equal to 2, the player will be sent to the northeastern quadrant. If it should be equal to 3, the player will be sent to the southern quadrant. Once the player has arrived at his/her particular mini-dungeon, his/her next objective is to reach the dungeon's inner sanctum. This is accomplished by reaching the exit at the far end of his/her mini-dungeon, which locates the player at the top entrance of the central quadrant. Then, the path to the inner sanctum is as simple as reaching one of the two exits in the area. See Figure 10-3 for a look at the treasure room.

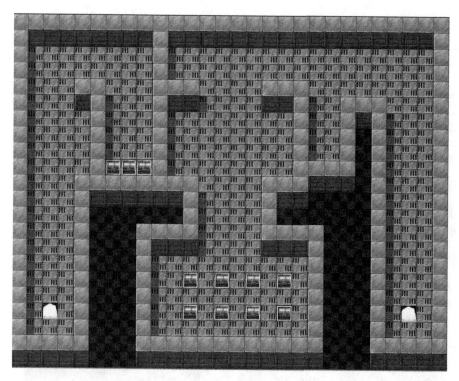

Figure 10-3. *The inner sanctum of the bonus dungeon. The left entrance is where the player arrives, if he/she takes the western exit out of the central quadrant. The right entrance is the player's destination if he/she takes the eastern exit*

You can place whatever items you like into those chests. Now, let's tweak the portal event a little.

A Random Portal

The previous event for the portal makes it so that it appears out of thin air at a specific location (mainly, wherever the event for the portal is placed). However, what happens if you want to place the portal within one of the dungeon levels? We could always place it at a static location, but we could also make it so that it spawns at a random location each time that it appears. For this exercise, let's use Level 5 as an example. I made a copy of the blank map and renamed it appropriately. Then, I set out to fix a basic problem. Think about this situation: you are the player and have received a message that a portal has materialized somewhere on the level. What happens if the portal spawns behind a wall or in the middle of an ocean? The player may not be able to reach it, and that is a big problem. How do we solve this problem? We can paint valid portal spawn locations with the Region tool and then check the portal's spawn position to make sure that it appears in a proper location.

199

Spawning the Random Portal

First of all, let's paint the land tiles in the blank dungeon level with Region #55.
See Figure 10-4.

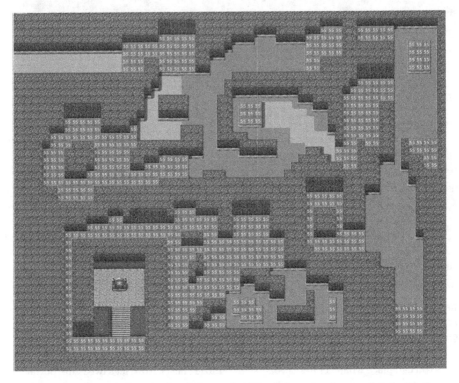

Figure 10-4. *The fifth dungeon level. Every tile of Dark Grass has been painted with the Region tool*

■ **Note**   Alternatively, you could have used a Terrain Tag to mark the appropriate tiles.

Once that is done, place the portal event we created previously in one of the map's
corners. Remove the switch conditional (such that the event is always visible). Then, let's
tweak the Parallel Process event. For the sake of simplicity, I won't be giving the portal a
finite life span, as I did in the previous section. Here's the Parallel Process event, now with
code to make sure the portal spawns in a valid location:

Page 1 of 2
```
@>Text: -, -, Normal, Bottom
:      : A portal materializes in the area!
@>Label: Repeat
```

```
@>Control Variables: [0023:PortalX] = Random No. (0...58)
@>Control Variables: [0024:PortalY] = Random No. (0...46)
@>Set Event Location: [Portal], Variable [0023][00024]
@>Get Location Info: [0018], Region ID, Variable [0023][0024]
@>Conditional Branch: Variable [0018:Region] != 55
  @>Jump to Label: Repeat
  @>
: Branch End
@>Conditional Branch: Variable [0018:Region] == 55
  @>Control Switches: [0020:PortalOpen] = ON
  @>
: Branch End
@>
```

Page 2 of 2
Condition: Switch 0020:PortalOpen is ON
Trigger: Action Button

The first thing to note is the addition of a pair of Control Variable event commands to set X and Y to random values. The range of numbers is set to the minimum and maximum limits of the map itself. That makes sure that the portal has to spawn on the map and prevents any possible bugs or glitches. After the event crunches X and Y, it moves the portal event to the relevant location. Then, through the use of Get Location Info, we determine whether the portal is on accessible land (marked by Region #55) or not (left unmarked). A pair of conditional branches handles what happens next. If the portal is on Region #55, we set PortalOpen to on, which stops the event from executing, by switching to a blank page 2. Otherwise, we jump back to the Repeat label and have the code re-randomize the portal's X and Y. This will keep repeating until the portal spawns in a legal location. Once the portal is on the map, it acts the same way as the portal we created in the last section (sending the player to one of three random mini-dungeons).

Quibbles

Of course, you've probably realized that the preceding logic has a few loopholes. Let's address them.

> **Problem:** There is a minute chance that the portal will spawn on top of the player.

> **Solution:** Compare the player's X and Y to the portal's location. If they are identical, re-randomize the portal's position. (Alternatively, you could move the portal one space away from the player, but that could render the portal out of bounds, complicating the issue).

Let's add the following lines to our Parallel Process event code. These lines go immediately after the `Conditional Branch: Variable [0018:Region] = 55` line.

```
@>Control Variables: [0019:X] = Player's Map X
@>Control Variables: [0020:Y] = Player's Map Y
  @>Conditional Branch: Variable [0019:X] == Variable [0023:PortalX]
    @>Conditional Branch: Variable [0020:Y] == Variable [0024:PortalY]
      @>Jump to Label: Repeat
      @>
    : Branch End
    @>
  : Branch End
```

The next line of code after that is the switch toggle for PortalOpen. What we do here is make sure that the portal is not on top of the player. If it is, we force the portal's position to re-randomize. Otherwise, we let the event conclude as normal.

> **Problem**: How do we get the portal to re-randomize if the player leaves the map and returns later?

> **Solution**: All that really has to be done is switch off PortalOpen. Keep track of every way that the player can leave the map and then add `Control Switches: PortalOpen = OFF` to each of them. When the player returns to the map, the portal will appear once again in a new location.

Handling Random Encounters with Common Events

Before moving on to another neat thing to add to your game, let's expand on what we learned concerning the Ancient Spirit's encounter, to create random encounters using common events in the extra dungeon. What we're going to do is make it so that, when an encounter is spawned, the game will pick from a list of enemy troops, instead of having a fixed encounter. This is easily done in one of two ways, both related to the Battle Processing event command.

1. Use the Designation with a Variable option, then have a variable that rolls a random number. The resulting number is then matched to the appropriate troop ID, and the correct battle is started.

2. Use the Same as Random Encounter option. In this case, you would set up the possible encounters in the Map Properties dialog menu and then limit their appearance to the proper Region.

During the course of this section, we will be using the first method. We will need two common events, much like before. The first one will be nearly identical to its counterpart in Chapter 9. Take a look below.

StepsToEncounter
```
@>Control Variables: [0010:StepsN] = 20
@>Control Variables: [0008:StepsTaken] = Steps
@>Script: n = $game_variables[10]
:       : $game_variables[9] = 18 + rand(n) + rand (n)
@>Control Switches: [0023:BonusDungeon] = ON
@>Call Common Event: [DungeonEncounters]
@>
```

It's pretty much identical to the StepsToAncientSpirit common event, with the sole differences being what switch is flipped on and what common event is called. You can use a two-line Autorun event on the dungeon map that calls the StepsToEncounter common event and then erases itself (via Erase Event) to prevent the game from hanging. The encounter event also shares some similarities with the Ancient Spirit's common event in the previous chapter. Take some time to look through it and see what's new and what's recycled.

DungeonEncounters
Trigger: Parallel Process
Condition Switch: 0023:BonusDungeon
```
@>Label: Restart
@>Control Variables: [0011:StepsTakenOnMap] = Steps
@>Control Variables: [0011:StepsTakenOnMap] -= Variable [0008:StepsTaken]
@>Conditional Branch: Variable [0011:StepsTakenOnMap] >= Variable
[0009:StepsToEncounter]
  @>Control Variables: [0019:X] = Player's Map X
  @>Control Variables: [0020:Y] = Player's Map Y
  @>Get Location Info: [0018], Region ID, Variable [0019][0020]
  @>Conditional Branch: Variable [0018:Region] == 1
    @>Control Variables: [0025:Troop] = Random No. (1...6)
    @>Jump to Label: Battle
    @>
  : Branch End
  @>Conditional Branch: Variable [0018:Region] == 2
    @>Control Variables: [0025:Troop] = Random No. (8...10)
    @>Jump to Label: Battle
    @>
  : Branch End
  @>Conditional Branch: Variable [0018:Region] == 3
    @>Control Variables: [0025:Troop] = Random No. (12...18)
    @>Jump to Label: Battle
    @>
  : Branch End
  @>Conditional Branch: Variable [0018:Region] == 4
```

```
      @>Control Variables: [0025:Troop] = Random No. (20...26)
      @>Jump to Label: Battle
      @>
    : Branch End
   @>Label: Battle
   @>Battle Processing: Variable [0025]
    : If Win
      @>Jump to Label: Resolve
      @>
    : If Escape
      @>Jump to Label: Resolve
      @>
    : Branch End
   @>
 : Branch End
@>Conditional Branch: Switch [0092] == ON
   @>Label: Resolve
   @>Control Variables: [0008:StepsTaken] = Steps
   @>Control Variables: [0010:StepsN] = 20
   @>Script: n = $game_variables[10]
   :       : $game_variables[9] = 18 + rand(n) + rand (n)
   @>Jump to Label: Restart
   @>
 : Branch End
@>
```

For starters, this common event is far longer than the Ancient Spirit equivalent, but that is due to the fact that we have to have one conditional branch for each of the regions on the map. Because we have four regions, we need four conditional branches to handle each of the distinct variable possibilities. Even so, I condense the code as much as I can, via the use of Labels. After all, why should I write the same Battle Processing command four times in a row when once will suffice? I check the player's x and y coordinates when an encounter is due, to see what region they are in, have the Troop variable roll a random number based on the encounters I want the player to face (they are all drawn from the main dungeon's enemy tables, but you could make new enemy troops for this dungeon), and then jump to the Battle label to handle the combat itself. Because these are meant to be regular encounters, I allow the player to escape. Whether the player wins or escapes the battle, the event jumps to the final (otherwise skipped) conditional branch and determines how many steps the player will have to take before being attacked once again. Afterward, the event jumps back to the top, ready to fire again when ready.

■ **Tip** You can use the Change Battleback event command to change the battle backgrounds of an area, based on the player's current Region.

Other Cool Things

In this final section of this final chapter, I will be covering several other cool things that you can do with what you have already learned during the course of this book.

Another Way to Randomize Chests

Remember when we initially discussed creating chests with random contents? We used a variable to roll a random number between one and ten. The player received an item based on the number rolled. Here's another way we can randomize chests to much the same effect. The difference, in this case, will be that we can specify the amount of items that the player will get as well. It's not as easy as it may seem, but it's not that difficult either. Your first idea might be to store a random number in a variable and use that within one of the Change event commands (Item, Weapon, or Armor). However, see Figure 10-5.

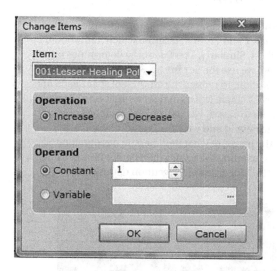

Figure 10-5. *The Change Items event command dialog menu*

Let's take Change Items as an example. As you can see, the item to be changed is fixed. What can be changed via a variable in the event command is the number of the item concerned. So, let's take a look at the Script Editor. Run a search for "Change Items," which should return a single result located in Game_Interpreter. Select it, and you should see the following code:

```
#------------------------------------------------------------------
# * Change Items
#------------------------------------------------------------------
  def command_126
    value = operate_value(@params[1], @params[2], @params[3])
    $game_party.gain_item($data_items[@params[0]], value)
  end
```

For the purposes of this exercise, we need only worry about the second line of this method. We can see that $data_items[@params[0]] is whichever item we select via the Change Items event command. And, we can infer that value is the quantity of that particular item to be added or taken away from the player's inventory.

So, with that said, if we wanted to have a chest that can give the player one of the first 14 items in the Database, we could have an event similar to the one below.

```
@>Control Variables: [0029:ItemRoll] = Random No. (1...14)
@>Control Variables: [0030:ItemQuantity] = Random No. (1...5)
@>Script: x = $game_variables[29]
:       : v = $game_variables[30]
:       : $game_variables[31] = $data_items[x].name
:       : $game_party.gain_item($data_items[x], v)
@>Text: -, -, Normal, Bottom
:       : You have obtained \V[30] \V[31](s)!
```

In the preceding event code, we use three variables to store relevant information. ItemRoll rolls a random number between 1 and 14, to determine which item should be given to the player upon opening the chest. Similarly, ItemQuantity determines how many copies of that item are given. Then, we use the Script event command to input some lines of code. I use variable substitution, to reduce the amount of space each line takes (whenever possible, it's best to have a single expression for a single line). I take a line to assign the name of the chosen item to $game_variables[31] and then execute $game_party.gain_item (using x for the item id and v for the quantity). Last, but definitely not least, we have to inform the player of what item he/she has obtained (and in what quantity). That's as easy as inserting the values of variables 30 and 31 into a Show Text event command. See Figure 10-6 for a sample execution of this code.

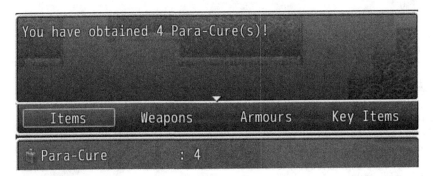

Figure 10-6. *The text box and inventory proof that the player has obtained the correct item in the correct quantities*

Logically, you can also apply this event code to weapons and armor, by using the appropriate parameter within $game_party.gain_item. That would be $data_weapons for weapons and $data_armors for armor. However, a cursory look at the $game_party. gain_item method as applied for weapons or armor will reveal an extra parameter. Let's take the Change Weapons script code as an example.

```
#-----------------------------------------------------------------
# * Change Weapons
#-----------------------------------------------------------------
  def command_127
    value = operate_value(@params[1], @params[2], @params[3])
    $game_party.gain_item($data_weapons[@params[0]], value, @params[4])
  end
```

After value, we have an extra parameter called @params[4]. This matches up with the Include Equipment check box in both Change Weapons and Change Armors and determines whether an equipped item can be taken, or only one that is in the player's inventory. This parameter should only be true if you want to take away a player's equipped weapon or armor (such as if he or she is fighting against a thief). For this example (as we're giving the player weapons/armor), we can always leave it as false.

Day-Night Cycle

While completely unnecessary in a dungeon crawler such as the game we created in the first nine chapters of this book, you can apply what you have learned during this chapter to add a day-night cycle to the game. There are several levels of complexity when it comes to day-night cycles.

- Time of day may only be changed by resting in specific locations or after certain story events.

- As stated it the previous bullet, time, too, is static while in towns but passes while on the world map.

- Additionally, time passes as the character moves, regardless of his/her current location.

As a matter of opinion, I think the best version of the day-night cycle is the one that only allows time to pass while the player is moving on the world map. We can make it so that inns move the clock to daytime or nighttime, to enable time-specific quests as well. For this exercise, I will create a pair of common events to handle the day-night cycle logic and a pair of torches that set the initial time of day when the player interacts with them. The completed result will look like Figure 10-7.

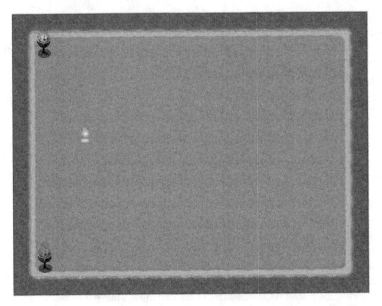

Figure 10-7. *The state of the map created for the day-night cycle exercise when completed*

At its core, a day-night cycle is little more than a Tint Screen effect and a flipped switch (to mark the current time of day, as it were). On that note, let's create our pair of torches. Each torch will turn on one of the two cycle switches and toggle off the other. Then, the screen will be tinted appropriately for the time of day. That will complete the bare minimum required for a day-night cycle. Naturally, I will expand on that a few times during this section.

Upper-Left Torch
Graphic: Red torch in !Other2
Options: Toggle Stepping Anim. Toggle Direction Fix
Priority: Same as Characters
Trigger: Action Button
@>Control Switches: [0026:Nighttime] = OFF
@>Control Switches: [0025:Daytime] = ON
@>Tint Screen: (0,0,0,0), @60, Wait

Lower-Left Torch
Graphic: Blue torch in !Other2
Options: Toggle Stepping Anim. Toggle Direction Fix
Priority: Same as Characters
Trigger: Action Button
@>Control Switches: [0026:Daytime] = OFF
@>Control Switches: [0025:Nighttime] = ON
@>Tint Screen: (-68,-68,0,68), @60, Wait

■ **Tip**   The Tint Screen values for daytime are the default numbers you see when initializing the Tint Screen event command (also accessible via the Normal button). The Tint Screen values for nighttime are the ones you get by clicking the Night button.

Not much to the basics, eh? Of course, you can get far more complicated than that. Now, let's say that you want to make it so that day turns to night (and vice versa) when the player has taken a certain number of steps (let's say 50). This is similar in premise to what we did with the Ancient Spirit. Here's the pair of common events needed to make time pass in the aforementioned manner.

Day-Night Cycle Start
Trigger: None
```
@>Control Variables: [0008:StepsTaken] = Steps
@>Control Switches: [0024:CycleON] = ON
@>Call Common Event: [Day-Night Cycle Logic]
```

Day-Night Cycle Logic
Trigger: Parallel Process
Condition Switch: 0024:CycleON
```
@>Control Variables: [0032:StepsToCycle] = Steps
@>Control Variables: [0032:StepsToCycle] -= 50
@>Conditional Branch: Variable [0032:StepsToCycle] >= Variable
[0008:StepsTaken]
  @>Conditional Branch: Switch: [0025:Daytime] == ON
    @>Control Switches: [0026:Nighttime] = ON
    @>Control Switches: [0025:Daytime] = OFF
    @>Tint Screen: (-68,-68,0,68), @60, Wait
    @>Control Switches: [0024:CycleON] = OFF
    @>Call Common Event: [Day-Night Cycle Start]
    @>Jump to Label: End
    @>
  : Branch End
  @>Conditional Branch: Switch: [0026:Nighttime] == ON
    @>Control Switches: [0026:Daytime] = ON
    @>Control Switches: [0025:Nighttime] = OFF
    @>Tint Screen: (0,0,0,0), @60, Wait
    @>Control Switches: [0024:CycleON] = OFF
    @>Call Common Event: [Day-Night Cycle Start]
    @>Jump to Label: End
    @>
  : Branch End
  @>
: Branch End
@>Label: End
@>
```

Before you read on, take a moment to add Call Common Event: [Day-Night Cycle Start] to both of the torch events. Now, let's discuss what's happening in those two common events. Selecting one of the two torches will start the sequence of events. We save the number of steps the player has taken to the StepsTaken variable. Then, we flip on the CycleON switch and call the Day-Night Cycle Logic common event. Why do I set the step count in the first common event, you may be wondering? It's pretty simple. If you want to count 50 steps, you need a baseline to start from. The easiest method is by using the Steps counter that RMVXA keeps internally. However, the only time that counter will be at 0 is when the player has just started a new game. Thus, we have to assign the step value to a variable and then modify *that* accordingly. If we had that variable assignment in the second common event, the time of day would never change.

Anyway, once CycleON has been triggered, we store the step value into a second variable called StepsToCycle and subtract 50 from that. Because the value of StepsTaken is static until otherwise called, this makes it so that there's a difference of 50 between StepsTaken and StepsToCycle. The conditional branch in the following line is executed once StepsToCycle is greater than or equal to StepsTaken. Naturally, that will happen in exactly 50 steps. There is then a pair of conditional branches that execute based on the current time of day. If it is daytime, the screen tint will become Night, the Daytime switch will be flipped off, and the Nighttime switch will be flipped on. If it is nighttime, the screen tint will become Normal, the Daytime switch will be flipped on, and the Nighttime switch will be flipped off. In either case, the CycleON switch will be flipped off, the Day-Night Cycle Start common event will be called, and a Jump to Label event command is used to prevent both conditional branches from executing in a single iteration. Otherwise, day would become night and then day in one single sequence, which is definitely unintended.

■ **Note**   You could also have a gradual transition—say, setting four levels of tint (maybe 0, -22, -44, and -68) and switching to those as the player's number of steps hits a certain threshold (every 15 steps or so), and then reversing it to change back to day. You might even put in some logic to, say, have 100 steps of daylight, then 50 steps of change, then 50 steps of nighttime, then 50 steps of change, and so on. You could even have it so that each step the character takes in the change period corresponds to a one-step change in the tint, so that the character sees a very gradual change in the light as it walks around.

Random Encounters in a Day-Night Cycle

So, now we have a day-night cycle that only requires the Day-Night Cycle Start common event to be called to start things off. Let's add another layer to the complexity by adding some random encounters to the map. First of all, we have to paint some Regions onto our map. I'm going to add three Regions. See Figure 10-8 for a screenshot of the map as displayed in Region Mode.

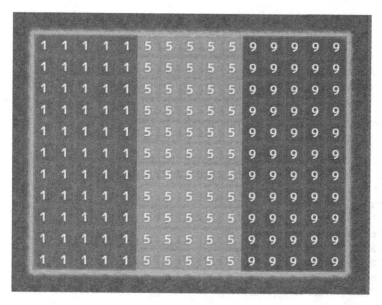

Figure 10-8. *A screenshot of our day-night cycle map in Region Mode*

Next, we have to create another pair of common events to handle the encounter logic on this map. The first encounter will serve a similar purpose to Day-Night Cycle Start, in that it will initialize the conditions for the second, more substantial, common event to work properly.

EncounterCall
```
@>Control Variables: [0033:CountToEncounter] = Steps
@>Control Variables: [0010:StepsN] = 20
@>Script: n = $game_variables[10]
:       : $game_variables[9] = 18 + rand(n) + rand(n)
@>Control Switches: [0027:EncountersON] = ON
@>Call Common Event: [CycleEncounters]
@>
```

This common event is laid out in much the same way as the StepsToAncientSpirit event. Since we already use StepsTaken for the day-night cycle, we have to use an alternate variable to hold the steps count for the start of the encounters common event. Why? It comes down to several problems that occur if we do not do this.

211

- Each phase of the day-night cycle lasts for 50 steps. The maximum possible roll for the encounter timer is 56 steps.

- If we were to use StepsTaken, its value would be reset each time day becomes night or vice versa. This would interfere with the correct processing of the encounter event. In the worst case scenario, you might not see a single encounter in an entire phase.

- Likewise, the encounter event would interfere with the day-night cycle in the same way.

Any way you slice it, this is an instance where not recycling certain variables will be for the best. Take a look at the following for the code for the encounter event.

CycleEncounters
Trigger: Parallel Process
Condition Switch: 0027:EncountersON
```
@>Control Variables: [0011:StepsTakenOnMap] = Steps
@>Control Variables: [0011:StepsTakenOnMap] -= Variable
[0033:CountToEncounter]
@>Conditional Branch: Variable [0011:StepsTakenOnMap] >= Variable
[0009:StepsToEncounter]
  @>Control Variables: [0019:X] = Player's Map X
  @>Control Variables: [0020:Y] = Player's Map Y
  @>Get Location Info: [0018], Region ID, Variable [0019][0020]
  @>Conditional Branch: Variable [0018:Region] == 1
    @>Control Variables: [0025:Troop] = Random No. (1...6)
    @>Jump to Label: Battle
    @>
  : Branch End
  @>Conditional Branch: Variable [0018:Region] == 5
    @>Control Variables: [0025:Troop] = Random No. (12...18)
    @>Jump to Label: Battle
    @>
  : Branch End
  @>Conditional Branch: Variable [0018:Region] == 9
    @>Control Variables: [0025:Troop] = Random No. (20...26)
    @>Jump to Label: Battle
    @>
  : Branch End
  @>Label: Battle
  @>Battle Processing: Variable [0025]
  : If Win
    @>Jump to Label: Resolve
    @>
  : If Escape
    @>Jump to Label: Resolve
    @>
  : Branch End
```

```
  @>
 : Branch End
@>Conditional Branch: Switch [0092] == ON
   @>Label: Resolve
   @>Control Switches: [0027:EncountersON] = OFF
   @>Call Common Event: [EncounterCall]
   @>
 : Branch End
@>
```

Take some time to compare this event with the DungeonEncounters common event we created for the bonus dungeon and note how I streamlined this one to the best of my ability. The last thing you will need to do is add Call Common Event: [EncounterCall] to both of the torch events. With that completed, we can call this section done! I urge you to figure out how to generalize the things covered in this section for use in a longer game. It's a great challenge, should you wish to accept it.

Achievements

To close out this final section, I'm going to cover achievements. In gaming terms, an achievement is a milestone that may or may not reward the player for reaching it. During the course of creating the dungeon crawler, we reward the player several times for advancing the main plot. However, what if we had a full-blown achievement system that detects when certain other milestones have been met? The common event below is meant to serve as a template that you can expand however you like. Without further ado, here it is:

Achievements
Trigger: Parallel Process
Condition Switch: 0041:AchievementsON
```
@>Control Variables: [0026:BattleCount] = Battle Count
@>Control Variables: [0027:PlayerLevel] = $game_party.members[0].level
@>Control Variables: [0028:TotalGold] = Gold
@>Conditional Branch: Variable [0027:PlayerLevel] >= 10
   @>Conditional Branch: Switch [0046:GetLevel10] == OFF
     @>Text: -, -, Normal, Bottom
     :     : You have reached Level 10!
     @>Control Switches: [0046:GetLevel10] = ON
     @>
   : Branch End
   @>
 : Branch End
@>Conditional Branch: Variable [0026:BattleCount] >= 10
   @>Conditional Branch: Switch [0042:Finish10Battles] == OFF
     @>Text: -, -, Normal, Bottom
     :     : You have completed your tenth battle!
```

```
    @>Control Switches: [0042:Finish10Battles] == ON
    @>
  : Branch End
  @>
: Branch End
@>Conditional Branch: Variable [0028:TotalGold] >= 1000
  @>Conditional Branch: Switch [0044:Get1000Gold] == OFF
    @>Text: -, -, Normal, Bottom
    :      : You currently possess 1000 Gold!
    @>Control Switches: [0044:Get1000Gold] == ON
    @>
  : Branch End
  @>
: Branch End
@>
```

■ **Note** $game_party.members[n] brings up the player character that's in position n-1 in the party. Thus, 0 marks the party leader. Given that we have made it so that the player cannot switch the position of the main character with that of his/her companion, 0 will always be either Palnor, Gust, or Feylia. From there, we can get his/her level with the expression listed above.

I did not include any actual rewards in these achievements, so feel free to add your own. Adding achievements to the game is as easy as flipping on the AchievementsON switch. I accomplished this by adding a green torch containing the necessary code to the character select map.

Page 1 of 2
Graphic: Green torch in !Other2
Options: Toggle Stepping Anim. Toggle Direction Fix
Priority: Same as Characters
Trigger: Action Button
```
@>Text: -, -, Normal, Bottom
:      : Would you like to turn on Achievements?
@>Show Choices: Yes, No
: When [Yes]
  @>Text: -, -, Normal, Bottom
  :      : Achievements enabled!
  @>Control Switches: [0041:AchievementsON] = ON
  @>
: When [No]
  @>
: Branch End
@>
```

Page 2 of 2
Condition: Switch 0041:AchievementsON is ON
Graphic: Green torch in !Other2
Options: Toggle Stepping Anim. Toggle Direction Fix
Priority: Same as Characters
Trigger: Action Button
```
@>Text: -, -, Normal, Bottom
:      : Would you like to turn off Achievements?
@>Show Choices: Yes, No
: When [Yes]
  @>Text: -, -, Normal, Bottom
  :      : Achievements disabled!
  @>Control Switches: [0041:AchievementsON] = OFF
  @>
: When [No]
  @>
: Branch End
@>
```

While achievements are disabled, the torch will offer to enable them. When achievements are enabled, the torch will offer to disable them. This covers the possibility of the player accidentally enabling them. Here are some other achievements you could add to the game:

- Achievements for killing a certain number of a certain enemy. This will require additionally that you increase the value of a variable when said enemy is defeated in battle.

- Achievements for number of steps taken

- Achievements for clearing optional content

Really, the sky is the limit when it comes to achievements! Feel free to take a look at your favorite games and see how players are rewarded in them.

Summary

During the course of this chapter, I have covered a variety of miscellaneous niceties that can be used to flesh out our dungeon crawler, including, but not limited to, creating a random shop, creating a portal that appears at a random location and takes the player to a bonus dungeon, and an achievements system. I would like to take a moment to congratulate you on making it to the end of this book. You now have a completed game to your credit, in addition to several other features that you can use to keep expanding the game. I humbly encourage you to continue learning about RMVXA and game design in general; it is quite a fascinating adventure! You can check out the Appendix to see links to helpful sites that will help you in your quest for knowledge. Otherwise, this is the end. In that case, I wish you the best of luck, and have fun!

■ ■ ■

Useful Resources for 2D Game Creation

This one and only appendix is a compilation of helpful resources that you can use for 2D game creation. In *Beginning RPG Maker VX Ace* (Apress, 2014), I used the appendix to provide various links related to the game-development engine mentioned in the title of that book. In this appendix, I do my best to prevent duplication between the links listed in each book and add some other links that will be useful for 2D game creation in general.

RMVXA Help Resources

This section lists links and references to tutorials and/or communities of people willing to help out aspiring RPG designers. Game design, like most things in life, is a constant process of renewing oneself and learning new ways to tackle old (and not-so-old) problems.

> http://forums.rpgmakerweb.com: This is the official forum for Enterbrain's video game development engines, including RPG Maker VX Ace.

> www.rpgmakerweb.com/support/products/tutorials: Also part of the official site. As the web link hints at, various tutorials perfect for beginners are located here.

> www.rpgmakervxace.net: One of the most populated unofficial forums related to RMVXA on the Internet. If you can't find the answer you're looking for on the official site, this should be your next destination.

> http://rpgmaker.net/tutorials/rmvxace: The site has more than 50 tutorials about various topics of interest in RMVXA.

■ **Note** On the official site for RPG Maker, you'll notice quite a few references to rpgmaker.net. Search engines will also steer you toward rpgmakerweb.com whenever they get a chance. Enterbrain has done a fairly good job of positioning itself as the universal destination for all things RPG Maker (which, given that they're the developers, is fair play). You can buy resource packs (music, art, etc.) from them, as well as a few other objects of interest.

---

www.amazon.com/Beginning-RPG-Maker-VX-Ace/ dp/1484207858: Here's a small measure of shameless self-promotion. My previously published book is perfect, if you're a beginner and want a robust reference to RMVXA. This particular link will send you to the paperback version of Beginning RPG Maker VX Ace. You can easily find the Kindle version once you land on Amazon.

Art Creation

Following is a pair of links to sites that cover how to create 2D sprites and pixel art. If you're of an artistic bent, this will help you do work in the 2D style of video game art.

http://2dwillneverdie.com/tutorial/: Contains a wide variety of tutorials for creating and manipulating 2D sprites. Pretty appropriate for a site called 2D Will Never Die.

www.petesqbsite.com/sections/tutorials/tuts/tsugumo/: Contains 11 tutorials for creating pixel art. The information within is more than ten years old, but still holds up.

Art Databases

On the other hand, perhaps you're *not* of an artistic inclination. Or, alternatively, you'd rather not spend your time creating art for your game. In that case, following is a pair of art databases that could serve your needs.

http://opengameart.org/: A site containing open source art, such as sprites and backgrounds. Make sure to check the licensing of each particular asset you decide to use in your own games, if you intend to go commercial.

http://freegamearts.tuxfamily.org/: As in the case of the previous link, this site also promotes the use and development of open source game resources.

Sounds and Music

No game is truly complete without an awesome soundtrack. A classic, retro-style game, for example, deserves an equally retro soundtrack. Here are some links to sites that host chiptune music (a.k.a. the music used in 8-bit games for consoles such as the Nintendo Entertainment System or NES).

> http://ericskiff.com/music/: Contains a link to a chiptune album called Resistor Anthems. The songs in the album are released under a Creative Commons Attribution License, so they are free to use for whatever purposes you can think of. The musician only asks that you notify him, so that he can link back to you.

> www.proudmusiclibrary.com/en/tag/8-bit/: There are exactly 39 8-bit songs hosted on Proud Music. You'll have to pay to license any of the songs from that site that you decide to use.

> http://pinkuboa.tumblr.com/post/92110744181/ see-i-did-do-something-for-200-followers-12: This particular Tumblr post does an awesome job of linking to a bunch of music resources that you can use for your own games—chiptune and otherwise (even going as far as pointing out that you shouldn't "steal music from published games and anime, use all this free stuff here instead!"). As usual, make sure to verify the licensing of a specific file before using it!

Fonts

Having a unique font can set your game apart. The Internet hosts many font marketplaces and sites, but following is one link in particular that caught my eye.

> www.1001fonts.com/retro+video-game-fonts. html?page=1&items=10: Contains 31 retro fonts. All of them are free for personal use, but only some are free for commercial use. Make sure you verify the usage rights for a specific font, if you wish to use them for commercial purposes.

Other Game Engines

RPG Maker VX Ace is hardly the only game-development engine on the market that can make 2D games. Here are three others:

> **Unity:** http://unity3d.com/unity/download—As the site link essentially states, Unity is a 3D game development engine. However, you can also make 2D games with it (see the next link), hence the reason I mention it here.

Unity 2D Tutorials: http://unity3d.com/learn/tutorials/modules/beginner/2d—Thirteen tutorials for 2D game development within the Unity engine are offered.

Construct 2: www.scirra.com/construct2—Construct 2 uses HTML 5 as its language of choice for the creation of 2D games.

GameMaker: Studio: www.yoyogames.com/studio—GameMaker has been around for quite a while and, much like RPG Maker VX Ace, can be used to make 2D games with only a minimum of programming experience.

Closing Notes

At the end of the day, it doesn't matter what game-development engine you use. While some engines lend themselves better to certain types of games (much like RMVXA works like a charm for RPGs), the most important part of making a game is actually designing it. The easiest game concept in the world is impossible to make for those who don't even bother trying! Take the knowledge you have gained from making this dungeon crawler and set forth. I wish you luck in all of your future endeavors!

Index

A

Ambush encounter
  locations, 128
  Parallel Process event, 129–130
  regions, 128
  RPGs, 127
Ancient Spirit
  screenshot, 179
  SpiritDamage and
    SpiritCurrentHP, 183
  StepsTakenOnMap, 180–182
  StepsToAncientSpirit, 179–181
  StepsToEncounter, 180
  troop event pages, 182–183
Ancient temple
  ancient artifact, 176
  barrier
    braziers, 173
    wall of fire, 175
  congratulations, 185
  enemies
    Dark Priests, 167, 170
    item drops and skills, 168
    Lost Archer, 167
    Lost Cleric, 167
    Lost Warrior, 167
    new skills, 169
  Great Escape
    Ancient Spirit
    (see Ancient Spirit)
    no return,
      yes escape, 183
  level, 166
  lost adventurers, 171

B

Bazaar
  achievements, 213–215
  chest randomization, 205–207
  day-night cycles
    levels of complexity, 207
    Logic common event, 209–210
    output, 207–208
    random encounters, 210
    StepsTaken and
      StepsToCycle, 209–210
    torches, 208
  dungeon crawler, 195
  NPC (see Nonplayer character
    (NPC)) portal
    Action Button trigger, 197
    creation, 195
    d3 variable, 197–198
    modulus operator, 196
    Parallel Process event, 195–196
    PortalCount, 196
    quibbles, 201–202
    spawning, 200–201
    StepsTaken, 196
    treasure room, 198–199
  random encounters, 202

C

Caves
  door
    annotations, 110
    blocking, 108
    gray switch event, 112

Caves (*cont.*)
    green switch event, 111
    iron events, 108
    red switch event, 110
    require key event, 107
  enemy encounters
    events process, 104–105
    item drops and skills, 101
    Kerberos action pattern, 103
    monsters, 100
    new skills, 101–102
    random roaming
      (*see* Roaming encounters)
    sprite, 103
  Kerberos, 120–121
  Lower Catacombs, transfer events, 99
  Magic Oar
    Chest Event, 118
    common event process, 116–117
    Dungeon tileset, 116
    Terrain Tags set, 116
  our game's Dungeon, 98
  random chests, 97
  town greeter, 98
  treasure
    chests characters, 113
    Database item, 114
    process, 113
    random chests event, 114
  vehicles, 97

D

d3 variable, 197
Dark Priests, 170
Day-night cycles
  levels of complexity, 207
  Logic common event, 209–210
  output, 207–208
  random encounters, 210
  StepsTaken and
    StepsToCycle, 209–210
  torches, 208
Dungeon crawler game
  lower catacombs (*see* Eagle's Crossing,
    lower catacombs)
  upper catacombs (*see* Eagle's
    Crossing, upper catacombs)

E

Eagle's Crossing
  lower catacombs
    enemy encounters, 85–87
    Living Statues, 94–95
    process, 81, 83
    puzzle creation, 88–91
    screenshot, 82
    town greeter, 82
    treasure room, 91–93
  population
    Equipment Shop, 61–63
    Item Shop, 72
    Magic Shop, 71
    Pub (*see* Pub population)
    Return Item creation, 75
    Return portal, 76
    town greeter, 79–80
    Weapon Shop event, 74
  upper catacombs
    blocking door event, 47
    chests selection, 53
    connections, 78–79
    damage formulas and spells, 41
    doodads, 37
    Erase Event, 47
    Event Tool, 39
    game progress, 38
    key creation, 39
    map-creating process, 37
    screen shot, 36
    Slime and Rat rewards, 45
    spell scrolls
      selection, 56–57
    stats and attack element, 45
    transfer events, 83–84
    treasure room, 50–52
    troops tab, 46
    types, 35
    wall tiles selection, 49
Enemy encounters
  catacombs
    events, 87
    item drop and skill, 85
    process, 85
    Salable Items, 86
    types, 85

Pixies' Forest
  added markings, 150
  ambush encounter
    (see Ambush encounter)
  hidden pixies, 153
  item drops
    and skills, 126
  Lamia, 148
  Magic Sail, 151
  Man-Eating Plant, 126
  new skills, 126–127, 149
  Orcs, 148
  paired encounters, 149
  rewards and skills, 148
  Sahagins, 148
  treasure, 156
Erase Event, 47

■ F

Feylia, 3

■ G

Gust, 2

■ H, I, J, K

Hidden dwellings, 145

■ L

Lost adventurers, 171

■ M

Magic Sail, 152

■ N, O

Nonplayer character (NPC)
  bazaar creation, 191–193
  event code, 193–194
  Shop Processing,
    Scripting Style
    goods variable, 188
    @index value, 188
    method definition, 188

  parameters, 190–191
  .push, 189
  RMVXA, 188
  Script Editor, 187, 189–190
  Shop Scene, 189
  while loop, 188

■ P

Palnor, 2
Pixies' Forest (East)
  dungeon level, 144
  enemy encounters
    added markings, 150
    hidden pixies, 153
    Lamia, 148
    Magic Sail, 151
    new skills, 149
    Orcs, 148
    paired encounters, 149
    rewards and skills, 148
    Sahagins, 148
    treasure, 156
  Lamia
    life, 161
    location, 157
    stock RMVXA graphic, 159
    troop event, 159
  level, 146
  player character, 145
  transfer events, 143, 146
Pixies' Forest (West)
  character-specific treasure, 142
  dungeon tileset, 124
  enemy encounters
    ambush encounter
      (see Ambush encounter)
    item drops and skills, 126
    Man-Eating Plant, 126
    new skills, 126–127
  normal treasure, 142
  Pixies' town (see Pixies' Vale)
  random treasure, 142
  transfer events, 124–125
  underground forest, 123
Pixies' Vale
  accessory shop, 139–140
  area surrounding, 130–131

Pixies' Vale (*cont.*)
  bullet list, 137
  exterior map, 134
  identical, 136–137
  interior map, 135–136
  Parallel Process, 134–135
  player interaction, 133
  portal to Eagle's Crossing, 140
  QueenTalk switch, 137, 139
  Return Crystals, 130
  Spiritual graphic set, 131–132
  Titania's event, 137–138
  Wall Vine graphic, 132–133
Portal's appearance, 195
Portal spawning, 197
Pub population
  events, 63–64
  companions
    dismissal NPC, 68–69
    Fighter and
      Apprentice classes, 65–66
    Innkeeper NPC, 70–71
    Wrendale's greetings, 66–68
Puzzle
  statues and gate, 89–91
  stone tablet, 88

■ Q

QueenTalk switch, 139
Quibbles, 201

■ R

Random encounters
  Battle Processing
    event command, 202–204
  events, 104–106
  RPGs, 103
  sprite, 103
Random portal
  quibbles, 201
  spawning, 200
Role-playing
  games (RPGs), 127
RPG Maker VX Ace
  (RMVXA), 188, 217–218

■ S

Stat system
  actor setting class, 19
  Armor creation, 24
  Bandit class, 18
  base class, 16
  character select system
    complete process, 27
    screen shot, 28
    source code, 29
    types, 26
  class level 99, 17
  equipment
    Armor and Helms game list, 21
    bow and arrow, 25
    Feylia staff weapons, 20
    game screenshot, 21
    pricing system, 22
    Warriors and Bandits
      weapons type, 19
  Mage class, 18
  Mage's HP curve, 17
  MHP and MMP class, 16
  sprite and portrait, 18
  Warrior class, 18
  weapon creation, 24
  weapon type, 25

■ T, U, V

2D game creation
  art creation, 218
  art databases, 218
  Construct 2, 220
  font, 219
  GameMaker, 220
  RMVXA, 217–218
  sounds and music, 219
  unity, 219
  Unity 2D Tutorials, 220

■ W, X, Y, Z

Weekend game framework
  blank maps, 13
  characters, 2
  Diablo, 1

Etrian Odyssey, 1
Eye of the Beholder, 1
leveling system work, 4
loot system work, 3
party-based/individual
    character game, 4
permadeath, 4
Rogue, 1
town of Eagle's crossing
    adventurer's quarter, 5, 12
    buildings, 5

Equipment Shop, 7
Magic Shop, 8
menu bar, 6
new map creation, 6
new project creation, 6
NPCs, 9
Parallel Process event, 11
pencil/square tool, 6
Pub, 8
transfer event, 9–10
verify RMVXA, 6

Get the eBook for only $10!

Now you can take the weightless companion with you anywhere, anytime. Your purchase of this book entitles you to 3 electronic versions for only $10.

This Apress title will prove so indispensible that you'll want to carry it with you everywhere, which is why we are offering the eBook in 3 formats for only $10 if you have already purchased the print book.

Convenient and fully searchable, the PDF version enables you to easily find and copy code—or perform examples by quickly toggling between instructions and   applications. The MOBI format is ideal for your Kindle, while the ePUB can be utilized on a variety of mobile devices.

Go to www.apress.com/promo/tendollars to purchase your companion eBook.